W9-DGY-643

TESL Canada Federation/Féderation TESL du Canada

President/Président
Shailja Verma

Vice-President/Vice-président
Jennifer Pearson Terell

Past President/Présidente sortante
Virginia Christopher

Secretary/Secrétaire
Christine Bertram

Treasurer/Trésorier
Deborah Yeager Woodhouse

Members at Large/Membres conseillers
Jacquelyne Lord
Bill McMichael
Jennifer St. John
Angela Schinas
Ron Thomson

Executive Director/Directrice exécutive
Louise Aerts

**TESL Canada Provincial Representatives/
Représentants provinciaux**
Esther Chassé (TESL Yukon)
Sarah ter Keurs (BC TEAL)
Phyllis Regier (ATESL)
Joyce Vandall (SCENES)
Tim MacKay (TESL Manitoba)
Barbara Krukowski (TESL Ontario)

Paula Lee Kristmanson (TESL New
  Brunswick)
Ellen Pilon (TESL Nova Scotia)
Paula Clark (TESL PEI)
Marcia Spence (TESL
  Newfoundland/Labrador

Address all correspondence to/Adresser toute correspondance à:
TESL Canada Journal/Revue TESL du Canada
408 - 4370 Dominion Street
Burnaby, BC V5G 4L7
Telephone: (604) 298-0312; 1-800-393-9199; Fax: (604) 298-0372
E-mail: admin@tesl.ca
Web site: www.tesl.ca

Acknowledgments/Remerciements

This publication is funded in part by the Language Acquisition Development Program of the Official Languages in Education Directorate, Canadian Heritage, under its program to encourage the dissemination of information on the teaching and learning of English and French as second languages. The University of Manitoba has also contributed to the *TESL Canada Journal* with institutional and professional support.

Cette publication est partiellement subventionnée par le programme de perfectionnement linguistique de la direction générale des langues officielles dans l'enseignement du patrimoine canadien, selon les termes de son programme qui vise à favoriser la diffusion de l'information sur l'enseignement et l'apprentissage du français et de l'anglais, langues secondes. La University of Manitoba a également contribué à la *Revue TESL du Canada* par son appui institutionnel et professionnel.

©TESL Canada Federation, 2006
ISSN 0826-435X
Printed in Canada

TESL Canada Journal/Revue TESL du Canada
Editorial Board/Comité de rédaction

Editor/Rédacteur en chef
John Sivell, Brock University

Joan Birrell-Bertrand, Editorial
Assistant
Naomi Stinson, Technical Editor
Dorine Chalifoux, Translator

Review Board/Comité consultatif

Patricia Balcom (TESL New
Brunswick)
Gulbahar Beckett (University of
Cincinnati)
Carmen Boulter (University of
Calgary)
Barbara Burnaby (Memorial
University)
Liying Cheng (Queen's University)
Nicholas Collins (BC TEAL)
Robert Courchêne (University of
Ottawa)
Ellen Cray (Carleton University)
Tracey Derwing (University of
Alberta)
Scott Douglas (University of Calgary)
Patricia Duff (University of British
Columbia)
Nick Elson (TESL Ontario)
Ruth Epstein (SCENES)
Antoinette Gagné (University of
Toronto)
Sheena Gardner (BAAL, UK)
Anita Girvan (Carleton University)
Sylvia Helmer (Simon Fraser
University)
Rebecca Hiebert (University of
Manitoba)
Jim Hu (Thompson Rivers University)
Jane Jackson (Chinese University of
Hong Kong)
Carla Johnson (University of Calgary)
Sandra Kouritzin (University of
Manitoba)
Icy Lee (Hong Kong Baptist
University)
Michael Lessard-Clouston (Biola
University, CA)

Guofang Li (SUNY Buffalo)
Xiaoping Liang (USC Long Beach, CA)
Xuemei Li (Queen's University)
Yi Li (University of Alberta)
Tim MacKay (TESL Manitoba)
Ardiss Mackie (Okanagan College)
Hedy McGarrell (Brock University)
Heather McIntosh (University of
Manitoba)
Bill McMichael (UBC)
David Mendelsohn (York University)
Bernie Mohan (UBC)
Brian Morgan, York University
Suhanthie Motha (University of
Maryland, College Park)
Murray Munro (Simon Fraser
University)
Garold Murray (Akita University,
Japan)
Eric Paulsoe (University of Calgary)
Ellen Pilon (TESL Nova Scotia)
Nathalie Piquemal (University of
Manitoba)
Hetty Roessingh (University of
Calgary)
Virginia Sauvé (ATESL)
Ling Shi (UBC)
Mark Tepunga (Ritsumeikan, Japan)
Ron Thomson (University of Alberta)
Gail Tiessen (Providence College)
Kelleen Toohey (Simon Fraser
University)
Carolyn E. Turner (McGill University)
Diana Turner (TESL Manitoba)
Deborah Yeager Woodhouse (Brock
University

Guest Reviewers

Carla Amaro
Shoaleh Bigdeli
Sandy Burger
Sara Cotterall
Bill Dunn
Charlotte Enns
Thomas Farrell
Yan Guo
Roumi Ilieva
Yatta Kanu

Masaki Kobayashi
Seonaigh MacPherson
Allan Meadows
Robert Renaud
Sylvie Roy
Karen Smith
Wayne Trotman
Hong Wang
Ying Zheng

Advertising Correspondence/Annonces publicitaires

Executive Director
TESL Canada Journal/Revue TESL du Canada
408 - 4370 Dominion Street
Burnaby, BC V5G 4L7
Telephone: (604) 298-0312; Fax: (604) 298-0372
E-mail: admin@tesl.ca

Editorial Correspondence/Correspondance aux éditeurs

Dr. John Sivell
TESL Canada Journal/Revue TESL du Canada
Dept. of Applied Linguistics (D350G)
Director, Centre for International Studies
Brock University
St. Catharines ON, Canada, L2S 3A1
E-mail: teslcan@ms.umanitoba.ca

The *TESL Canada Journal* is indexed in Canadian Education Index.
La *Revue TESL du Canada* est répertoriée dans le *Répertoire canadien sur l'education.*

TESL Canada Organizations/Organisations du TESL Canada

Yukon
c/o Elaine Hurlburt
Box 5403
Haines Junction, Yukon Y0B 1L0

Alberta
c/o Department of Educational Psychology
6-102 Education Centre North
University of Alberta
Edmonton, AB T6G 2G5

Manitoba
TESL Manitoba Membership
c/o Manitoba Teachers' Society
191 Harcourt Street
Winnipeg, MB R3J 3H2

New Brunswick/Nouveau-Brunswick
c/o TESL Certification
Faculty of Arts
University of New Brunswick
PO Box 5050
Saint John, NB E2L 4L5

**British Columbia/
Colombie-Britannique**
BC TEAL Membership
201 - 640 West Broadway
Vancouver, BC V5Z 1G4

Saskatchewan
SCENES Membership
PO Box 176
Lunsden, SK S0G 3C0

Ontario
TESL Ontario Membership
27 Carlton Street, Ste 405
Toronto, ON M5B 1L2

Nova Scotia/Nouvelle-Écosse
TESL Nova Scotia Membership
PO Box 36068
Halifax, NS B3J 3S9

Newfoundland/Labrador/Terre-Neuve
TESL NFLD/LAB Membership
PO Box 254, Station C
St. John's, NF A1C 6K1

Editorial Policy

TESL Canada Journal, established in 1984, is a fully refereed journal for practicing teachers, teacher educators, graduate students, and researchers. *TESL Canada Journal* invites the submission of unpublished manuscripts concerning the teaching and learning of official languages; second-language teacher education; and the maintenance and development of minority, heritage, or Aboriginal languages.

Categories of Publication

Full-Length Articles. Articles in this category advance conceptual, research-based, or theoretical arguments, fully grounded in current literature. Manuscripts should normally not exceed 7,000 words excluding references. A maximum 100-word abstract must be included. *In the Classroom.* Articles in this category feature descriptions of teaching techniques or activities within a theoretical framework. Articles should specify audience, materials, procedures, and teacher reflections on procedures. Manuscripts should not exceed 3,500 words excluding references.

Perspectives. Submissions to this section are of the following types: (a) reactions of readers to articles and reviews published in the journal and rejoinders; (b) viewpoints and opinions expressed in the form of a report, commentary, or interview on issues or topics of current interest; (c) the text of plenary keynote addresses; (d) review articles of one or more influential books in the field of TESL in the light of current theory and pedagogy. *Perspectives* submissions should not exceed 3,500 words. *Reviews. TESL Canada Journal* publishes short evaluative reviews of print and nonprint materials relevant to TESL professionals. Potential reviewers may contact the editors if they wish to review any of the books listed in each edition of the Journal.

Required Style

Manuscripts not conforming to the guidelines set forth in the *Publication Manual of the American Psychological Association*, 5th edition, may be returned for adjustment prior to review. The *TESL Canada Journal* welcomes articles from non-native speakers of English or French, but would ask that ideas be clearly expressed.

Submission

All manuscripts will be screened to ensure that the name(s) of the author(s) cannot be identified in the manuscript. To facilitate the review process, the editors ask that manuscripts be sent: (a) by e-mail attachment to the e-mail address above or (b) on a high-density diskette with hard copy included to the mailing address above.

The preferred formats are Microsoft Word for Windows or Microsoft Word for MacIntosh.

Manuscripts should be labeled by the first author's last name, dot, ms (e.g., smith.ms) and should include the title, abstract, text, acknowledgments, notes, and references. A separate attachment labeled by the first author's last name, dot, info (e.g., smith.info) should list the title of the manuscript, name(s) of the authors, and complete information for the contact author including both e-mail and regular mail addresses. A maximum 50-word biographical note should be included for each author.

When manuscripts are accepted, authors will be asked to submit electronic or disk versions, in camera-ready format, of all diagrams or tables. Obtaining permissions to reprint previously published material is the responsibility of the author(s).

Manuscript Changes

The editors reserve the right to make minor editing changes without prior consultation with the author(s). Authors will be contacted regarding any major editing or revisions.

Languages of Publication

English and French.

Politique de la rédaction

Fondée en 1984, la *Revue TESL du Canada* est une revue avec comité de lecture anonyme pour les enseignants, les formateurs d'enseignants, les étudiants des cycles supérieurs et les chercheurs. La *Revue TESL du Canada* accepte les manuscrits inédits portant sur l'enseignement et l'apprentissage des langues officielles; la formation d'enseignants de langue seconde; et le maintien et le développement de langues minoritaires, ancestrales et autochtones.

Catégories de publications

Articles de fond. Les articles de cette catégorie proposent des arguments conceptuels, théoriques ou empiriques, tous appuyés par la recherche courante. Les manuscrits ne devraient pas, normalement, dépasser 7 000 mots sans compter les références. Un résumé d'une longueur maximale de 100 mots doit accompagner le manuscrit.

En classe. Dans cette section, les articles présentent des descriptions de techniques ou d'activités d'enseignement dans un cadre théorique. Ces textes devraient fournir des précisions sur les participants, le matériel et les démarches accompagnées de réflexions de l'enseignant sur celles-ci. Les manuscrits ne devraient pas dépasser 3 500 mots sans compter les références.

Perspectives. Cette section est consacrée à quatre types d'articles : (a) la réaction des lecteurs aux articles et aux comptes rendus qui ont paru dans la revue et, le cas échéant, la réplique de l'auteur; (b) des opinions et des points de vue présentés sous forme de comptes rendus, de chroniques, ou d'entrevues touchant des sujets d'actualité; (c) les discours de séances plénières; et (d) des comptes rendus de livres d'influence touchant un domaine de la revue, rédigés à la lumière de la pédagogie et des théories actuelles. Les textes soumis ne devraient pas dépasser 3 500 mots.

Comptes rendus. La *Revue TESL du Canada* publie de brefs comptes rendus évaluatifs visant les enseignants d'anglais langue seconde. Si vous désirez faire la critique d'un des livres de la liste publiée à la fin de chaque numéro de la revue, contactez les éditeurs.

Exigences de la présentation

Les manuscrits qui ne respectent pas les exigences du manuel *Publication Manual of the American Psychological Association* (5ᵉ édition) pourraient être retournés à l'auteur pour modification avant d'être évalués. La revue accepte des articles d'auteurs dont la langue maternelle n'est ni l'anglais, ni le français, mais exige que les idées soient bien exprimées.

Soumission de manuscrits

Une vérification de tous les manuscrits est effectuée pour s'assurer que l'identité de l'auteur ou des auteurs n'y est pas révélée. Pour faciliter le processus d'examen, veuillez envoyer votre manuscrit, soit par courriel comme pièce jointe à l'adresse ci-dessus, soit sur une disquette à haute densité avec une copie imprimée à l'adresse postale ci-dessus. Employez, de préférence, Microsoft Word pour Windows ou MacIntosh. Sur votre manuscrit, indiquez le nom de famille du premier auteur, suivi d'un point et de ms (p.ex. tremblay.ms). Un titre, un résumé, vos remerciements, et des notes et références bibliographiques devraient accompagner le manuscrit. Dans un texte séparé et étiqueté ainsi : nom de famille du premier auteur suivi d'un point et info (p.ex. tremblay.info), indiquez le titre du manuscrit, le nom de l'auteur ou des auteurs et les coordonnées de l'auteur principal (y compris l'adresse électronique et postale). Veuillez inclure des notes biographiques d'une longueur maximale de 50 mots pour chaque auteur. Aux auteurs de manuscrits acceptés on demandera une version électronique ou sur disquette de tous leurs schémas et tableaux, prêts à photographier. L'auteur est responsable d'obtenir la permission de faire réimprimer des documents qui déjà été publiés.

Révision des manuscrits

Les éditeurs se réservent le droit d'apporter des corrections mineures aux manuscrits sans consulter l'auteur au préalable. En cas de révisions ou de changements majeurs, le ou les auteurs seront contactés.

Langues de publication

Anglais et français

TESL Canada Journal
Revue TESL du Canada

Vol. 24, No. 1, Winter/Hiver 2006

Contents/Matières

Book Reviews/Comptes rendus

Books for Review, Winter 2006

Oxford Advanced Learner's Dictionary with Compass CD-ROM (7th ed.), 2005
Literacies: Researching Practice, Practicing Research. Tannis Atkinson, November 2003
Latino Language and Literacy in Ethnolinguistic Chicago. Marcia Farr, 2005
Teaching English to the World: History, Curriculum and Practice. George Braine, 2005
Sociocultural Contexts of Language and Literacy (2nd ed.). Bertha Perez, 2004
Contextualizing College ESL Classroom Praxis: A Participartory approach to Effective Instruction. Lawrence N. Berlin, 2005
Situational Context of Education: A Window into the World of Bilingual Learners. Maria Estela Brisk, Angela Burgos, and Sara Ruth Hamerla, 2004
Review of Adult Learning and Literacy (Vol 4) Connecting Research, Policy and Practice. John Comings, Barbara Garner, and Cristine Smith, 2004
Conflicting Paradigms in Adult Literacy Education: In Quest of a U.S. Democratic Politics of Literacy. George Demetrion, 2005
A Glossary of Morphology. Laurie Bauer, 2004
Language, Literacy, and Power in Schooling. Teresa L. McCarty, 2005
Oxford Basics Activities Using Resources. Heather Westrup and Joanna Baker. 2005

Teaching and Learning Vocabulary: Bringing Research to Practice. Elfrieda H. Hiebert and Michael L. Kamil, 2005

A Word From the Editor

This is my first editorial for the TESL Canada Journal. In it I would like first of all to thank Sandra Kouritzin for the highly cooperative way in which she managed the change-over of Editors. There is a lot to learn about this job—indeed I'm painfully aware that the learning process is still not entirely complete—but Sandra had an exceptionally accurate sense of what I needed to know first and of how much I could assimilate at a given moment. So I am glad to say that the transition was relatively panic-free. Thank you very much, Sandra.

No doubt that feeling of comfort and continuity was promoted as well by the fact that Joan Birrell-Bertrand, who had already developed admirable skills as Sandra's editorial assistant, agreed to continue with me too, which I very much appreciate. And now, my goodness, here we are at the end of preparing our first issue of the Journal together, and so far Joan has not yet given up on me!

All the articles for this issue were received, reviewed, and approved for publication under Sandra's editorship, with the final copy-editing shared between Sandra and myself. This issue of the Journal will be a little longer than usual, which provides an opportunity to present our readers with an especially abundant offering of research, reflection, and thought-provoking commentary on the state of our profession in a variety of domains.

Robert Pinet explores features of the LINC 4 & 5 Curriculum Guidelines that seem to promote diverse models of newcomer integration, whereas Michelle Szabo examines the use of standard or nonstandard language forms by L2 learners as a reflection of individual sociocultural identity. An innovative approach to Content-Based Instruction is proposed in the article by Martha Bigelow, Susan Ranney, and Anne Dahlman. Su-Ja Kang documents the interaction of individual and contextual factors as influences on the language-learning process of a Korean physician. Yan Guo discusses how schools can encourage and recognize varied forms of involvement by parents in their ESL children's educational experience. A practical and theoretical question of importance to many ESL or EFL teachers is addressed by JoEllen Simpson: how to provide the most effective feedback on students' writing. And in an ambitious study conducted at four universities in France, Nathalie Piquemal and Robert Renaud report on the combination of integrative and instrumental motivations influencing students' foreign language learning progress. Finally, in the In the Classroom section, Justine Light gives an enlightening personal account of professional growth through engagement in the process of participatory education as practiced in a community-based ESL program. At the end of the volume, you will find reviews of two interesting books—both on aspects of sociolinguistics—by Joan Birrell-Bertrand and Ellen Pilon.

This brief overview highlights not only the richness of the work that is being done in our field overall, but also the quality and diversity of the manuscripts submitted to the *TESL Canada Journal* in particular. And in that connection, it is appropriate to comment on the immensely valuable service provided to the Journal by its Review Board and guest reviewers. With such a variety both of topics and of research methods, it is essential for the Journal to be able to rely on the skills of reviewers with collectively very broad expertise. Reviewing is a demanding and time-consuming responsibility, and the Journal simply could not succeed without this resource. Throughout the process of copy-editing, which in part entails following up on responses to suggestions by reviewers, I was time and again deeply impressed by the precision, care, and tact with which feedback had been provided. It may seem to be a bit of a cliché to say that our profession is a community, but at times like this, it becomes clear that the claim is entirely justified.

I am looking forward to my term as Editor of the *TESL Canada Journal*. The future is bright. Past Editors have led the Journal to a position of considerable respect; promising new manuscripts continue regularly to reach us for review. Moreover, along with this copy of the Journal you will receive an invitation to participate in a reader satisfaction survey that will help assure that what "ain't broke will not get needlessly fixed" and that what might be improved will indeed receive attention.

John Sivell

Un mot de l'éditeur

Ce texte constitue mon premier éditorial pour la *Revue TESL Canada* et je tiens à remercier Sandra Kouritzin pour sa façon très collaborative de gérer le changement d'éditeurs. Il y a beaucoup à apprendre sur ce travail, et je suis bien conscient que mon apprentissage n'est pas encore terminé. Cependant, Sandra a fait preuve d'un sens exceptionnellement précis quant à ce que je devais savoir en premier et combien d'information je pourrais assimiler d'un moment à l'autre. Je peux donc affirmer que la transition s'est accomplie presque sans panique et j'en remercie sincèrement Sandra.

Si je me sens si à l'aise dans mon nouveau poste et si j'ai cette impression de continuité, c'est sans doute aussi attribuable au fait que Joan Birrell-Bertrand, qui avait déjà eu l'occasion de développer ses capacités admirables en tant qu'assistante à la rédaction pour Sandra, a accepté de continuer à travailler avec moi. Je lui en suis très reconnaissant. Nous voilà déjà en train d'achever la préparation du premier numéro de la Revue sur lequel on collabore et Joan ne m'a pas encore laissé tomber!

Tous les articles dans ce numéro ont été reçus, évalués et acceptés pour la publication alors que Sandra était encore éditrice. Sandra et moi avons partagé le travail de la vérification et la mise au point finales des copies. Ce numéro étant un peu plus long que d'habitude, il vous offre une lecture particulièrement étoffée portant sur des recherches, des réflexions et des commentaires touchant divers domaines de notre profession.

Robert Pinet se penche sur des aspects du programme-cadre CLIC 4 & 5 qui semblent promouvoir divers modèles d'intégration des nouveaux arrivants. Pour sa part, Michelle Szabo étudie l'emploi, par des élèves en ALS, de formes standard et non standard en tant que reflet d'une identité socioculturelle individuelle. L'article de Martha Bigelow, Susan Ranney et Anne Dahlman propose une approche novatrice à l'enseignement basé sur le contenu. Su-Ja Kang décrit l'interaction de facteurs individuels et contextuels qui jouent un rôle dans l'apprentissage L2 d'un médecin coréen. Yan Guo explique comment les écoles peuvent reconnaître et favoriser diverses formes d'implication par les parents dans l'éducation en ALS de leurs enfants. L'article de JoEllen Simpson traite d'une question importante, aussi bien sur le plan pratique que théorique, pour les enseignants en ALP ou ALS : Comment fournir la rétroaction la plus efficace sur les rédactions des élèves? L'étude ambitieuse de Nathalie Piquemal et Robert Renaud entreprise dans quatre universités en France porte sur la combinaison de motivations intégratives et instrumentales qui influencent les progrès en apprentissage d'une langue étrangère par les étudiants. Dans la section *En classe*, Justine Light présente un récit personnel enrichissant qui décrit sa participation dans la pédagogie active d'un programme communautaire d'ALS et l'épanouissement professionnel qui s'en est suivi. Ce numéro conclut avec les comptes-rendus de Joan Birrell-Bertrand et Ellen Pilon qui font la critique de deux livres intéressants portant sur des aspects de la sociolinguistique.

Ce bref survol souligne à la fois toute la richesse du travail qui s'accomplit dans notre domaine de façon générale et la qualité et la diversité des articles soumis à la *Revue TESL Canada* en particulier. À propos, il est pertinent d'évoquer le service immensément important que rendent à la revue le comité d'évaluation et les auteurs des comptes-rendus de livres. Compte tenu de la grande diversité de sujets traités et de méthodologies de recherche employées, il est essentiel que la revue puisse avoir recours aux habiletés de critiques dont l'expertise recouvre une gamme très étendue. Évaluer des manuscrits est une responsabilité qui exige beaucoup de temps, et une tâche essentielle à la réussite de la revue. Pendant la vérification et la mise au point de la copie, qui en fait découle en partie des suggestions des évaluateurs, j'ai à maintes reprises été très impressionné par la minutie et le tact des commentaires des évaluateurs sur les copies. Dire que notre profession est une communauté peut sembler stéréotypé, mais dans un contexte comme le nôtre, je peux affirmer que l'expression est tout à fait juste.

J'entrevois avec anticipation mon mandat comme éditeur de la *Revue TESL Canada*. L'avenir s'annonce bien : mes prédécesseurs ont fait en sorte que la revue s'attire maintenant beaucoup de respect et de nouveaux manuscrits prometteurs continuent à nous parvenir. De plus, vous recevrez avec cette copie de la revue, un sondage sur le niveau de satisfaction des lecteurs dont le but est de nous aider à maintenir ce qui va bien et porter notre attention vers ce qui pourrait être amélioré.

John Sivell

JOHN SIVELL

The Contestation of Citizenship Education at Three Stages of the LINC 4 & 5 Curriculum Guidelines: Production, Reception, and Implementation

Robert Pinet

This article highlights how citizenship and citizenship education are sites of contestation. I have analyzed the process of curriculum making of the LINC 4 & 5 Curriculum Guidelines (TCDSB, 1999) through three stages: from production, through reception, to implementation. The production stage is investigated by contrasting commentaries from two members of the Advisory or Specialist Committees who helped to prepare the document. The reception stage featured a thematic analysis of the Guidelines. The implementation stage is investigated through interviews with five present or former LINC teachers, who discuss how they used or are using the Guidelines as part of their curriculum-in-use. Although this LINC document can be characterized as representing a "Liberal democratic" approach to citizenship and a transactional approach to citizenship education in a multicultural framework, a minority position supporting a more critical and transformational approach to citizenship education is also evident.

Cet article souligne que la citoyenneté et l'éducation à la citoyenneté sont des notions qui prêtent à la contestation. L'auteur a analysé le développement, en trois étapes, du programme-cadre d'études CLIC 4 et 5 (TCDSB, 1999) : production, accueil et mise en oeuvre. L'étude de l'étape de la production repose sur la comparaison de commentaires de la part de deux membres des comités consultatifs ayant participé à la préparation du document. Celle de l'étape de l'accueil a consisté en une analyse thématique du programme-cadre. Pour l'étape de la mise en oeuvre, l'auteur s'est appuyé sur des entrevues avec cinq enseignants de CLIC (anciens ou actuels) portant sur l'emploi qu'ils faisaient, ou avaient fait, du programme-cadre dans leurs cours. Alors que le document CLIC se caractérise par une approche libérale et démocratique à la citoyenneté et une approche ponctuelle à l'éducation à la citoyenneté dans un cadre multiculturel, une position minoritaire appuyant une approche plus critique et transformationnelle à l'éducation à la citoyenneté s'en dégage également.

Introduction

Studies of the federally sponsored Language Instruction for Newcomers to Canada (LINC) program have tended to focus on mini-ethnographies of small groups of language settlement teachers (Cray, 1997; Cleghorn, 2000; Richardson, 1999) or of textual analysis of citizenship concepts (Thomson & Derwing, 2004). In this study, I analyze one curricular text from LINC through the three stages of production, reception, and implementation.

I begin by introducing various concepts of citizenship and citizenship education through a literature review. Then I offer a brief history of the federally funded LINC language and settlement program for immigrants. Next, using Miller and Seller's (1990) model of three types of curriculum—transmission, transaction, and transformation—I show how various interpretations of citizenship education inform the production, reception, and implementation stages of the *LINC 4 & 5 Curriculum Guidelines*. Each stage represents a site of conflict in which the formalized descriptors of a task-based, communicative language document both enable and constrain the types of citizenship practices that might be explored through pedagogy.

The production stage is investigated through data provided by two members of the Expert or Advisory Committees involved in the curriculum-making process, the reception stage through a thematic analysis of the document, and the implementation stage through interviews with five present or former LINC teachers who discuss how they used, modified, or ignored the *Guidelines* while acting as curriculum-makers in their own LINC classrooms.

Theoretical Framework: Curriculum Metaorientations

Miller and Seller's (1990) *Curriculum: Perspectives and Practice* offers a model of three characteristic types of curriculum metaorientations—transmission, transaction, and transformation—which differ in context, aim, learning experience, role of the teacher, and evaluation.

In a transmission curriculum, the context is based on an atomistic paradigm in which reality is broken down into distinct elements. Transmission is linked philosophically to empiricism, psychologically to behaviorism, and politically to conservatism. The aim of transmission is subject mastery and the inculcation of social norms. Students are expected to learn facts and concepts in a structured environment where the teacher plays a directive role and where evaluation is based on traditional achievement tests.

Bobbitt's (1924) education theory of the 1920s and 1930s is a prime example of transmission curriculum (Miller & Seller, 1990). It is based on the breaking down of subject matter in a school curriculum into small components that mirrored the mechanistic society and sought to shape the individual student to social norms. In *How to Make a Curriculum*, Bobbitt (1924) stresses practical and conservative aims for education. In a chapter on objectives, he writes, "But merely shifting positions is not necessarily progress. There are more ways of going wrong than of going right. The status quo is usually better than changes in the wrong directions" (p. 7).

The application of "scientific" principles to increase efficiency (while maintaining the status quo of early 20th-century America) is also apparent in the list of 821 Major Objectives of Education, which take up 19 pages of the third chapter of Bobbitt's book (1924). One of the subsections is devoted to "Efficient Citizenship." Objective 201 reads, "Ability to think, feel, act, and react as an efficient, intelligent, sympathetic and loyal member of the social group—that group that is prior to differentiation and within which social differentiation occurs" (p. 15). By this Bobbitt suggests that loyalties to particular identities should be subsumed in citizenship education to loyalty to the (apolitical or) greater society. Or more particularly, in terms of the citizenship education of immigrants, that they are to lose their ethnic identities in the social melting pot of the United States. The transmission model has been attacked by critical theorists for aiming to conserve and reproduce existing social structures.

A transaction curriculum stresses interaction between the student and the social environment. It is linked psychologically to cognitive developmentalism and politically to liberalism. The aim of a transaction curriculum is to develop rationality and complex problem-solving skills. The learning experiences stress inquiry and the development of both problem-solving skills and "inquiry skills that facilitate democratic decision making" (Miller & Seller, 1990, p. 110). The teacher plays the role of facilitator in this type of curriculum metaorientation by stimulating inquiry by asking probing questions. Evaluation focuses on the student's acquisition of complex intellectual frameworks and social skills.

Dewey's theory of education (in books published from 1897 to 1952) serves as a prime example of a transactional curriculum. For Dewey, education, "by employing the scientific method, can help direct the course of social change in a positive direction" (Miller & Seller, 1990, p. 63).

Rooted in the scientific method, the student moves through a five-step process by: (a) confronting a problematic situation; (b) defining exactly what the problem is; (c) clarifying the problem through analysis; (d) developing hypotheses; and (e) selecting one hypothesis and implementing it. This method, which Dewey (1931) labeled the "'project,' 'problem' or 'situation,' was to serve as an alternative "to organization of courses on the basis of adherence to traditional divisions and classifications of knowledge" (p. 30). Dewey wrote:

> There cannot be a problem that is not a problem of something, nor a
> project that does not involve doing something is a way which demands
> inquiry into fresh fields of subject matter ... Another feature of the
> problem method is that activity is exacted ... Within the limits set by
> capacity and experience this kind of seeking and using, of amassing and
> organizing, is the process of learning everywhere and at every age. In
> the third place, while the student with the proper "project" is

intellectually active, he is also overtly active; he applies, he constructs, he expresses himself in new ways. He puts his knowledge to the test of operation. (pp. 33-35)

Dewey believed that education was "the fundamental method of social progress and reform" (1897, "My Pedagogical Creed," Article V). His was a liberal philosophy in that he believed "that in the ideal school we have the reconciliation of individualistic and the institutional ideals"; socialistic because he recognized that "right character is not to be formed merely by individual precept ... but rather by the influence of a certain form or community life upon the individual ... and that the social organism through the school, as its organ, may determine ethical results."

The transformational curriculum has as its context the ecological paradigm in which all phenomena are linked. It is tied psychologically to transpersonal psychology and politically to movements for social change. Its aim is "self-actualization, self-transcendence, [and] social involvement" (Miller & Seller, 1990, p. 167). Learning experiences focus on the integration of many dimensions, including the physical, cognitive, affective, and spiritual, and on making connections between disciplines, inner and outer realities, and the school and community. Teachers must be in touch with their inner lives, have developed their communication skills, and strive to make links between their classrooms and the larger community. Evaluation is often informal and experimental.

The transformation position, according to Miller and Seller (1990), is represented by two currents of thought, one romantic or humanistic and the other neo-Marxist and concerned with educating for social change. The romantic (or transpersonal) current stresses equality between teacher and child, play and unstructured activity, intrinsic motivation, and a focus on spirituality and the interconnectedness of all reality. Major writers on the romantic current of transformational curriculum include Rogers (1969), Maslow (1970, 1971), and Wilber (1983).

The social change position of transformational curriculum is exemplified in the work of Paulo Freire and Henry Giroux, among others. These theorists see curriculum as a locus of conflict, as a site of contestation. Freire's (2001) three-step procedure of *consciencisão* (consciencization) involves naming important conflicts in a community's situation and "generating interest in these key words," thus enhancing literacy; analyzing the "systemic causes of conflict" in the community; and encouraging "collaborative action to resolve conflicts" (Miller & Seller, 1990, p. 160). This "pedagogy of the oppressed"

Must be forged with, not for the oppressed (whether individuals or people) in the incessant struggle to regain their humanity. This pedagogy makes oppression and its causes objects of reflection by the oppressed, and from that reflection will come their necessary engagement in the struggle for their liberation. And in this struggle this pedagogy will be made and remade. (p. 48).

By stressing the integration of the personal and the political, by helping peasants to become conscious of the social, political, and economic roots of their poverty and illiteracy, and by moving students from self-understanding to social involvement, Freire's curriculum is a prime example of a social change transformational curriculum.

In essence, then, emancipatory pedagogy is a pedagogy of social change. Where transaction curriculum is student-centered and stresses individual engagement, transformational pedagogy seeks the transformation of society as a whole, either in an evolutionary (transpersonal) or revolutionary (emancipatory) manner.

According to Giroux (1983), if emancipatory citizenship education

is to be emancipatory it must begin with the assumption that its major aim is not "to fit" students into existing society; instead, its primary purpose must be stimulate their passions, imaginations, and intellects so that they will be moved to challenge political, and economic forces that weigh so heavily upon their lives. (p. 351)

In this article, I use the transmission, transaction, and transformation paradigms to analyze various positions of citizenship education.

Citizenship and Citizenship Education

Citizenship and citizenship education are highly contested concepts. In a review of citizenship education in public schools in Canada, Sears and Hughes (1996) offer two tables that identify four major conceptions of citizenship and citizenship education. They indicate how ideas about sovereignty, government, and the role of citizens can range from the implicit to the explicit, and how these then inform an equally broad range of ideas about knowledge, values, and skills/participation in citizenship education.

Each conception in Sears and Hughes' (1996) proposed typology "illustrates a view of what constitutes good citizenship and the corresponding knowledge, values, and skills students must learn to be good citizens" (p. 126). Interestingly, Sears and Hughes' models of citizenship education mesh with Miller and Seller's (1990) definitions of curriculum metaorientations.

In Conception A, students are taught a common body of knowledge about the nation's history and political structures. Political and military history are taught in a context of a "narrative of continuous progress" (Sears & Hughes, 1996, p. 128). Institutions are presented as operating in a lockstep fashion, and teaching styles are traditional. Students are taught a set of national values and the skills needed to vote in an informed manner. This is similar to the characteristics of Miller and Seller's (1990) transmission curriculum, with its focus on facts, concepts, mastery of school subjects, and teacher-directed classroom activity. The aim is to reproduce the curriculum as it is from generation to generation.

In Conception B, "students learn the knowledge necessary to become involved in resolving public issues" (Sears & Hughes, 1990, p. 128). This knowledge is drawn from the liberal arts. Liberal democratic institutions are presented as the best form of social organization in theory, but as flawed in practice. Teaching styles focus on students arriving at alternatives in order to resolve social issues through critical reflective practices and cooperation. This model shares many characteristics with Miller and Seller's (1990) trans-action curriculum, with its emphasis on inquiry and problem-solving skills used to facilitate democratic decision-making.

In Conception C, the focus is on preparing citizens of the world. Students are taught about world systems and global topics in order to become com-mitted to ecological responsibility and social justice. They develop critical thinking and cross-cultural skills. In Conception D, a more critical approach is favored. Students are taught that institutions and social structures create oppressive social conditions and to value equality and confront privilege and inequality. These last two conceptions of communitarian citizenship educa-tion mirror the two tendencies found in transformational curricula. Concep-tion C mirrors Miller and Seller's (1990) romantic-ecological type of transformation, which stresses the interdependence of phenomena and is linked with self-actualization, mysticism, and worldwide environmental movements, whereas Conception D adopts the social-change position in its emphasis on consciousness-raising and community-based political action.

Although Sears and Hughes (1996) maintain that, at least in their official documentation, citizenship education in public schools in Canada reflects an activist position, Derwing (1992), basing her analysis of 200 responses to a citizenship instruction survey sent to citizenship and/or ESL programs across Canada in 1987 (Derwing & Munro, 1987), asserts that adult im-migrants receive a citizenship education that inculcates passivity. Derwing maintains:

> the predominant view [of] … citizenship is static … seen as something
> to be acquired rather than a process of continuous growth in attitudes,
> skills, and knowledge. The nature of *The Citizenship Act* serves to
> encourage a minimal approach to citizenship instruction in that
> citizenship and ESL programs generally react to the limited knowledge
> and language criteria stated therein. (p. 193)

In fact, "86 percent of respondents cited preparing students for the [Citizen-ship] Court hearing as the main objective of their programs" (p. 197). Thus the vast majority of the teachers and administrators in the citizenship and/or ESL programs surveyed by Derwing and Munro (1987) transmitted concepts of citizenship as a series of facts to be memorized by students for their citizenship hearings.

It is clear that Derwing (1992) understood citizenship education in the programs she surveyed in 1987 to be based on a transmission (or Conception A) approach to citizenship education. In its place, she calls for a more transactional (or Conception D) curriculum that will stress developing immigrants' inquiry and critical skills. "How we treat citizenship education is a reflection of what we believe citizenship to be. We encourage passivity by denying people the opportunity of developing the knowledge and/or the skills to participate actively in society" (p. 201).

A brief review of the literature of ESL and citizenship courses for immigrants in Canada reveals that many analysts seem biased in Derwing's direction, in being critical of the role of ESL teachers for promoting passive citizenship to immigrants. Bullard's (1989) analysis of citizenship education programs in the 1980s points out that, "by and large, materials and methodologies used in citizenship classes are directed at helping students meet the requirements for naturalization and prepare for their interview with a citizenship judge" (p. 21).

Referring the Derwing and Munro study (1987), Bullard (1989) states that most programs then were "delivered outside the context of ESL, in the form of short-term courses providing information about Canada's geography, history, and political system in order to help applicants meet the knowledge requirements for the citizenship hearing" (p. 24).

It is the development of critical thinking skills among immigrants to Canada, through the use of critical language awareness, that most concerns Morgan (1995/1996). In his article "Promoting and Assessing Critical Language Awareness," Morgan stresses the community basis of many ESL programs in Toronto and believes that a critical community-based ESL pedagogy must include "organizing and assessing second language education around experiences that are immediate to students" (p. 11). Morgan's article is important for highlighting critical language perspective, which he describes as follows.

> Dominant social groups ... rely upon the power of language to
> normalize ways of seeing, knowing, and doing that support their
> particular interests and privileges. But consent is never a foregone
> conclusion. Words and texts have many potential meanings ultimately
> mediated by the particular experiences of the language users ...
> Language is used to put people in their place; people also use language
> to change where they've been placed. (p. 12)

This brief review of the literature points to a tendency among many ESL analysts to disparage much citizenship education for instilling a passive absorption of rote citizenship facts. In contrast, these authors promote the use of critical language awareness as a tool for helping immigrants develop critical and reflective problem-solving and cross-cultural skills so that they can participate more effectively as Canadian and world citizens.

A Brief History of LINC and the Canadian Language Benchmarks

The federal government, in its Immigration Plan for 1991-1995, placed a new emphasis on providing "services at all stages of settlement, from pre-arrival to citizenship," including the creation of the Language Instruction for New-comers to Canada program (Bettencourt, 2003, p. 25) The provisions of the program were laid out in two documents, *Innovations in Training* and *New Immigrant Language Training Policy*, but were later modified in Ontario after consultations with community-based groups from February to June 1992. LINC was established to provide immigrants with basic communication skills, a learning environment that took into account new developments in curricula, teacher orientation, and methodologies (Bettencourt, 2003; Cray, 1997).

The *Draft LINC Curriculum Guidelines* outline "12 themes, including family life, transportation and Canadian society, for three different levels with tasks, grammar, vocabulary, and pronunciation points that can be taught [as well as] a LINC literacy curriculum" (Cray, 1997, p. 33). The guidelines were designed to meet the needs of students "in a variety of community and institutional settings and to specify content, method, and approach for LINC classes."

In 1997, *Revised LINC Curriculum Guidelines* (LCRT Consulting, 1997) were published, again for LINC 1 to 3. In the following year, "the Toronto Catholic District School Board [TCDSB] was awarded the contract to develop the curriculum guidelines for LINC 4 and 5 ... to establish measurable outcomes based on the Canadian Language Benchmarks" (TCDSB, 1999, p. 9). The TCDSB published the *LINC 4 & 5 Curriculum Guidelines* in 1999.

In 2001, Citizenship and Immigration Canada contacted the TCDSB "to combine the two existing curriculum guidelines for LINC and make them consistent with the *Canadian Language Benchmarks 2000*" (Witol, 2004, p. 15). The result, the *LINC 1-5 Curriculum Guidelines*, were published in 2002.

This article is concerned with the *LINC 4 & 5 Curriculum Guidelines* (TCDSB, 1999) because it was the guideline document used by the participants in this study when they worked as LINC teachers. Furthermore, initial access to one of the two members of the Expert or Advisory Committees involved in the planning of these guidelines allowed me to investigate this curriculum document from its planning stages through to its subsequent use by these teachers.

The Canadian Language Benchmarks

Although LINC provides a specific curriculum for teachers in this language and settlement program, it is the Canadian Language Benchmarks that are used to assess the language level of immigrants across English-speaking Canada so that they can be placed in appropriate LINC class levels.

The first assessment tool used with LINC was A-LINC, developed at Vancouver Community College in 1992 (Bettencourt, 2003). In 1992, Employment and Immigration Canada

> funded a project to develop national standards, beginning with consultations with experts in second language teaching and training, testing and measurement. The consultations confirmed that no one instrument, tool or set of "benchmarks" was widely used or appropriate to Canadian newcomers' needs. (Pawlikowska-Smith, 2000, p. vi)

In March 1993, the National Working Group on Language Benchmarks (NWGLB) was established by Citizenship and Immigration Canada. This group published the first version of the Canadian Language Benchmarks in 1996. A revised version, *Canadian Language Benchmarks 2000*, followed.

The Benchmarks are

> a descriptive scale of communicative proficiency in English as a Second Language (ESL) expressed as 12 benchmarks or reference points; a set of descriptive statements about successive levels of achievement on the continuum of ESL performance; [and] statements (descriptions) of communicative competencies and performance tasks in which the learner demonstrates application of language knowledge (competence) and skill. (Pawlikowska-Smith, 2000, p. viii)

The Benchmarks are used by assessors in LINC assessment centers to place immigrant students in the proper LINC level.

In the following section, I analyze how various concepts of citizenship and citizenship education inform the *LINC 4 & 5 Curriculum Guidelines* through three stages: in its production, reception, and implementation.

The LINC 4 & 5 Curriculum Guidelines: The Production Stage

In "The Practical: Translation into Curriculum," Schwab (1973) outlines a deliberative form of curriculum planning in which representatives from five disciplines—the subject matter, the learners, the milieus, the teachers, and the curriculum specialist—collaborate with one another through a two-phase process. In the first phase, these representatives or "agents of translation" go through a three-step program of *discovery, coalescence*, and *utilization*, to generate "new educational materials and purposes" (p. 501).

Each representative is to be treated as an equal participant in the col-laborative process, in order to discover the experiences of others and for a coalescence to occur of these bodies of experience in the curriculum-making process. The curriculum specialist must not seek to overawe the group, but rather should serve three functions: first, in the preliminary or discovery phase, to remind the group of the importance of the experience of each representative; second, in the writing or coalescence stage, to administer the process of the realization of the curriculum; and third, in the revision or utilization stage, through the trial use and reworking of this curriculum.

The creation of the curriculum guidelines for LINC 4 & 5 appears to have followed Schwab's (1973) deliberative model. In the development of the *Guidelines*, there were three committees, the Guidelines Advisory Commit-tee, the Guidelines Expert Panel, and the Ontario Region LINC Advisory Committee (ORLAC), which reacted to the curriculum at various stages. As well, piloting of the guidelines was done with various groups of teachers and a survey taken of LINC teachers who had used the *Guidelines.*

Thus representatives of the five disciplines mentioned by Schwab (1973) were involved in this curriculum-making project: the subject matter (English-as-a-second-language and settlement issues) through specialist ad-visers, the learners (the immigrant students), the milieus (cultural advisors, schools, school boards), and the teachers (through field testing, question-naires, and workshops).

Comments by two informants, members of the Expert or Advisory Com-mittees, highlight the fact that the process of making the *LINC 4 & 5 Cur-riculum Guidelines* was one of contestation as well as compromise. One informant stated,

> There was considerable debate around the issue of technology in the
> Guidelines (important for integration into Canadian society) the
> organization of the material in the Guidelines to offer the teachers that
> maximum amount of flexibility—organizing the material around
> themes with the material for LINC levels 1-5 being inserted
> consecutively rather than all the material for the 12 themes at each LINC
> level being presented separately.

Whereas this informant raised concerns about the role of technology, teacher flexibility, and the ordering of the thematic material in the *Guidelines*, the other's concerns focused on some of the difficulties involved in trying to deal with two related issues—form-based instruction and content-based in-struction—while also trying to provide for the possibility of a more critical citizenship pedagogy given the constraints imposed on it by the LINC 1-3 guidelines and the task-based Canadian Language Benchmarks.

According to this second informant, the Canadian Language Benchmarks are underpinned by two theoretical components, Krashen's acquisitional model of language learning and Nunan's framework for task-based learning. For Nunan (1989),

> A communicative task is a "piece of classroom work involves learners in comprehending, manipulating, producing, or interacting in the target language while the attention is principally focused on meaning rather than form. The task should also have a sense of completeness, being able to stand alone as a communicative act in its own right." (Fox & Courchêne, 2005, p. 7)

This informant's goal was to justify theoretically the introduction of pre- and post-tasks into the curriculum, in order to "move towards explicit ... grammatical and pronunciation components" and thus legitimize what many ESL instructors had already been doing with their immigrant students. As well, this informant was concerned with focusing on content in a more critical way in each of the thematic components. This was highlighted in a discussion about the theme of banking.

> Banking can mean two things, you know: are banks ethical or moral, or how do I open a banking account? And I worked very hard to make sure that both elements were in the units. I said, "Let's do banking, but one of the topics is going to be what are the ethical limits of ... bankers. Is it moral, what they're doing?" And stick that in there right beside how do I open a checking account ... That we don't take things at face value. That we look at every topic and unit from both sides.

In terms of the curriculum metaorientations, this informant's efforts can be seen in the framework of attempting to include more transactional aims and learning experiences in a curriculum document the antecedents of which had tended to stress the transmission approach of survival English, focusing on facts and concepts required by immigrants for their citizenship interviews.

Exception was also taken by this informant in how the Canadian Language Benchmarks equate students' abilities to analyze complex social issues with their abilities to communicate and analyze opinions.

> One of the things I tried to talk about ... [was] how, even at a basic level, people will engage with the substance of these topics, but they will frame them in everyday experience ... It's an elitist attitude, when the curriculum's like that. When they get to Level 12 and they can manipulate this highly complex sentence structure, then they can talk about human rights, or the Canadian political system which, you know, I think is nonsense. And I used to complain bitterly to people in the writing of documents that this doesn't need to be that way.

Critical citizenship was characterized as involving "a kind of critical autonomy ... the ability to not take things at face value, to appraise and evaluate … To be able to weigh the consequences and to see whose interests are being served behind anything and whose are not." Although admitting that some of the themes could not be developed in the *Guidelines* given the restrictions imposed on the team by the Canadian Language Benchmarks, this informant is still pleased that the document does provide LINC teachers with possibilities for critical engagement about citizenship.

> I think that there [are] really positive aspects of the document. Just the fact that they are there encourages teachers … the fact that it's there allows teachers who feel they want to do that kind of teaching, who are inspired by it … [to be] legitimated to do it … I think it's a great document and, for those people who want to build on it, I think the basic tools are there.

This informant's analysis of the curriculum development process of the *LINC 4 & 5 Curriculum Guidelines* reveals that deliberation did take place, during which a range of opinions about both more explicit language teaching as well as various conceptions of citizenship and citizenship education were presented and discussed.

The LINC 4 & 5 Curriculum Guidelines: Reception—The Written Form

A note from the *Guidelines* serves as an apologia to those seeking content geared toward a more critical approach to citizenship education and lays the responsibility for its lack on the task-based focus of the Canadian Language Benchmarks.

> Using the Canadian Language Benchmarks to develop these curriculum guidelines imposes certain limitations. Competencies that may be more suitable to particular topics could not be used because they do not correspond to the Benchmarks assigned to LINC 4 and 5. For example, International Human Rights, Native Peoples and National Unity do not lend themselves easily to the pragmatic, functional competencies described in the CLB at these levels and are more suited to competencies such as critical analysis (Reading, Benchmark 9) or expressing and analyzing opinions (Listening/Speaking, Benchmark 8). Consequently, these topics may not have been addressed as profoundly as the issues warrant but were included anyway because learners expressed an interest in them. (TDCSB, 1999, p. 10)

The *Guidelines* present 12 themes, each divided into three parts: Business, Canada, Canadian Culture and Society, Canadian Law, Community and Government Services, Education, Employment, Finance and Banking, Global Issues, Health and Safety, Relationships, and Travel and Tourism (TCDSB,

1999). Analysis reveals that sample language tasks do range, on occasion, from the pragmatic to the more critical. For example, under Canada—Government, topic outcomes include the ability of students to "describe systems of government in Canada and other countries" as well as to "agree, disagree with current government policies" (p. 35). The topic Canada—Native Peoples has as an outcome to "relate a story about a famous Native Canadian" (p. 37), and a suggestion is also made that "Classes might want to learn about recent court cases involving Native claims to ancestral lands and natural resources" (p. 36). Other critical aspects of the text either in terms of suggestions, topic outcomes, or sample language tasks include writing "a short text about [students'] own experience with Canada's multicultural society" (Canadian Culture and Society—Cultural Diversity, p. 39); "legal definitions of child abuse; legal requirements to report child abuse ... legal supports for women who are victims of domestic violence; the legal rights of same-sex couples" (Canadian Law—Family Law, p. 46); "barriers to employment for immigrants; discriminatory practices by professional organizations" (Employment—Skills Assessment, p. 66); and "the social and ethical responsibility of banks and government regulatory bodies; the implications of bank mergers" (Finance and Banking, p. 68) are a few instances.

The LINC 4 & 5 Curriculum Guidelines: Implementation—The Curriculum-in-Use

Participants
Besides the two informants from the Expert or Advisory Committees, I also interviewed five present or former LINC teachers with whom I was working or had already worked, one man and four women with a total of 58.5 years' teaching experience among them (or over 10 years' experience each, on average). Three of the five had taught adults exclusively for school boards and in colleges in the Toronto area, as well as for a Toronto-area college with an arrangement to take students from China. Besides teaching LINC 1, 3, 4, and 5, these teachers had also taught adult ESL in the Labour Market Language Training program, in a Toronto-area school board program, English for Academic Purposes, as well as French and Italian. One of the teachers had spent each alternate school year teaching kindergarten to grade 6 in a public school.

Study
Within institutional guidelines for free and informed consent, I interviewed the participants between October and December 2002 in various settings. Interviews were audiotaped and then transcribed. In the interviews, I focused on how each participant dealt with what he or she considered the more controversial themes or his or her more controversial duties in LINC. It

was here especially that the demarcation between those who favoured a mixed transmission/transactional approach, a mixed transactional/transformational approach, or a purely transformational approach became more readily apparent.

Data and Findings

Transmission pedagogy. None of the participants followed a "pure" transmission approach to curriculum.

Transmission/transaction pedagogy. Three of the five teachers interviewed felt comfortable teaching practical themes. As one teacher explained, "I feel more comfortable teaching the themes that I thought they would use, such as shopping … [or] health care services." Another voiced similar sentiments when she noted, "In level 4 and 5, it was also very functional, so we taught things about buying and selling, negotiating things, on top of the regular housing in Canada and all that regular citizenship stuff." A third mentioned how his students considered information related to Canada important.

> Because when you teach Canada, they perceive that, in a way, as an academic thing. Or it's very clear to them that they have to amass some kind of information about this new country. Also, that's a very varied topic, since you're teaching this province, geography, history. So I think they enjoy that.

Teachers mentioned that they tailored their classes to meet the majority of their students interests, as one class may be made up primarily of adult immigrants who have been professionals in their country and are interested in getting a Canadian job as quickly as possible, to either older people or housewives who are not looking to work, but rather come to class for social and academic reasons. As one teacher mentioned,

> I think looking for work, Canadian culture and geography [were popular] … Those are the main ones … Because, in one class, I had a lot of professionals, and they all wanted to go out and work. I had engineers … You know, I accommodated it to the class. The other class I had, the 4 high, were only interested in just studying a little bit of geography—a lot of women that weren't working and didn't intend to work. So just general knowledge … You know, different levels of government, different newspapers we have to read, what the climate is like here, how many provinces we have. All that kind of stuff.

These teachers taught practical topics using a more transmission-oriented pedagogy, often centered around form-based grammatical points.

> So … I would model the grammar point, and then I would try to use authentic materials from the community that had the structure. So I would get maybe brochures from the Canadian Human Resources

Centre and we would look at the grammar structure there, or we would look at sample interviews. That, to me, was the most important ... that LINC was authentic material, because they [students] would have to use these materials and if they could see the structure, then they might be able to use it.

Other authentic activities these participants mentioned using included having students fill out forms, write résumés, and role-play job interviews.

Conversely, when faced with teaching a more controversial topic, such as women's rights or same-sex issues, most participants seemed to react by ignoring the topic completely or else by allowing students a limited amount of time for a values' clarification discussion. The topic that made three of the teachers the most uncomfortable was same-sex issues. Two avoided the issue altogether. As one explained, "Same-sex benefits and things like that, I strongly believe in, but with quite a few Muslim students, any mention of topics like that made the women very uncomfortable." Creating a nurturing environment was important to this teacher, and controversial topics that might divide the class were best not debated, because "I just didn't want them [students] to be uncomfortable. I wanted them to feel they could come and learn and not justify their religious views and things like that."

A second participant seemed to have mixed feelings about not wanting to confront a controversial topic like homosexuality. She likened dealing with cross-cultural sensitivities to walking a tightrope because, "You have to be careful. You don't want to offend people, but, at the same time, you know, you want ... to keep them interested in learning. That's why they're there."

At the same time, this teacher became intrigued by a colleague's willingness to discuss this issue with her students. Visiting her colleague, this participant found vocabulary about homosexuality on the board and asked this teacher how she had broached the subject.

And she said, "Oh, yeah. I'm talking about differences in the family and what we accept." And there was something else she did ... some vocabulary ... She did much more than me, in that. And that's when I started to think, "I never thought about that."

Thus this teacher became aware of new pedagogical ways to broach delicate subjects in a multicultural classroom.

Two participants defused the same-sex issue by resorting to a legal interpretation of rights for homosexuals in the framework of Canada's liberal-democratic system. This exemplifies Sears and Hughes's (1999) Conception A of citizenship education, in that teachers teach "a particular set of national values." One teacher expressed the view that although everyone was entitled to his or her opinion on the subject, in the end, "It doesn't matter who you are or what you are, the law says this. And this is the way it should be." Another revealed that she would say, "that I could understand where they were coming from, but, you know, now they are in Canada."

A more transactional response to the topic of women's rights saw some participants pose Socratic questions or engender small-group discussions in order to generate values clarification among their students. The participant who did not deal with homosexuality did deal with women's issues as "a positive, not as a negative, as in: 'We've done this ... and this is what happens in other countries.'" Faced with a male student's misogynistic claim that "women aren't smart," this participant asked questions, "so that they would be able to debate back and forth. Or explain their justification ... The right questions ... will elicit responses from them and get them to think, you know, 'What if? What if?'" Another male participant responded to the views expressed by a group of Middle Eastern male students about women by encouraging discussion. These men believed that their culture protected women, "because women were all covered up in the traditional dress and protected by the family and [could not] walk in public," whereas "we put half-naked women all over advertisements, and I think they mentioned the porn industry." This participant continued,

> I think I discussed it with them, that this was news to me, that, actually, somebody sees what happens in the Arabic world and what we perceive as repression ... they perceive as protection. And I didn't just discard the idea. I thought, "Hum, this is something to think about!"

In the end this teacher agreed with the men about the fact that sexual exploitation of women existed in the West, but suggested that other movements existed at the same time that were trying to change the situation. "I didn't defend our culture," this participant went on, "as the ultimate and superior and totally perfect, all the problems have been solved ... I admitted that yeah, we have both [situations] here, I guess. And we're working on it."

This approach, of admitting to how Western society fell short of its own ideals, is reminiscent of Sears and Hughes' (1990) Conception B of citizenship education, because in this instance, liberal democracy was "presented as the best theoretical form of social organization but as flawed in practice" (p. 128).

Transformational Pedagogy

Only one of the five teachers interviewed used the *Guidelines* as part of a transformational pedagogy in an effort to promote "self-actualization, self-transcendence, [and] social involvement" (Miller & Seller, 1990, p. 167). This participant had been involved in the LINC program since one year after its inception in 1992 and had taught some LINC 2, but mainly LINC high 3 classes, which she believed was equivalent to a low LINC 4 class in that, "You can take any subject that is in LINC 4 or 5 curriculum and teach it to the LINC 3 high."

The *Guidelines* themes this teacher used consistently were "human rights, job search, the law in Ontario and education issues in Ontario," but it is in her combination and critical use of these themes that this participant's pedagogy can be understood as transformational. She connects "human rights and ... workers' rights to any kind of employment stuff they are going to do" in order to expose her students to some of the hidden discriminatory practices at play,

> because a lot of our students believe that there is no racism, that there is no sexism, that these things exist somewhere, but it's not going to affect them. So I bring in some of the ideas, not to frighten them and I tell them that, "I hope I haven't upset your world, but I want you to know that this exists, and this is how it works."

As an example, she mentioned distributing newspaper stories dealing with various discriminatory situations. One dealt with a major electronics chain's policy of not promoting nonwhites to management positions, an attempt by three white managers to change the head office's policy, the company's firing of one of the managers, and this manager's subsequent challenge before the Ontario Human Rights Tribunal. The students moved from learning about a local company, "a company they would patronize" and its racist promotional policy, to the fact that "management became responsible to the workers and to each other for what was going on." Next, through simplified authentic material, students studied the Ontario Human Rights Code. Then students were asked if they had experienced these kinds of things in their own countries. They began "by totally denying" it. Later, students were asked to identify a situation that they or someone they knew had experienced when they first arrived in Canada that they had not realized had been a form of discrimination at the time. The students were then encouraged to write about this, then give an oral or dramatic presentation, which involved "all the competencies." Students then offered peer reviews of these presentations based on pronunciation and other discrete items.

This participant believed strongly that

> the settlement part of the LINC program has to be confrontational and heads-on. I think you need to show people that what they're facing is real. It's not in their heads. It's not just because they've just gotten here. It may go on for years.

At the same time, she also believed that a lot of LINC teachers "pussy-foot around the negative, and I think that is unfair and it's not giving these people a fair chance" to deal with the systemic forms of racism and sexism they face as immigrants to Canada.

This participant's form of transformative pedagogy is closely related to Sears and Hughes' (1996) Conception D of citizenship education, which stressed consciousness-raising and community-based political action.

Limitations of the Study

Although I have sought to analyze the concepts of citizenship that have informed the making, final form, and implementation of the *LINC 4 & 5 Curriculum Guidelines*, I would be remiss not to acknowledge certain limitations to my study. For example, although I was fortunate in being able to interview one informant and receive feedback from another, both of whom had been members of Expert or Curriculum Guideline Committees, my study would have benefited from input from other members of the Expert Panel, the Curriculum Guidelines Advisory Committee, teachers' groups, or the writing team. This would have helped create triangulation and a clearer sense of the contestation around citizenship on these committees. Also, my study could be faulted for being based on interviews with five teachers who are, or have been, my colleagues in various schools in the Toronto area.

Conclusion

This article highlights how citizenship and citizenship education are sites of contestation. Although the LINC document analyzed here can be characterized as representing a liberal democratic approach to citizenship and a transactional approach to citizenship education in a multicultural framework, a minority position supporting a more critical and transformational approach to citizenship education is also evident.

Unlike Derwing's (1992) findings in which teachers stressed that their main function was to aid adult immigrants pass their Citizenship Test, these teachers' objectives tended to center on teaching students about Canada and wanting to help them participate in Canadian society and improve their English. What varied among the participants in this group was the type of participation the teachers' envisaged for their students. Most wished to aid them in their settlement process so that they might become citizens active in Canadian society; at least one envisaged her students being both socially active and critically aware.

Although this work, like many qualitative studies, deals with only a small group of participants, I believe it can help shed light on how curriculum-making and use are processes of contestation and adaptation. As well, I hope it will encourage LINC teachers to develop a critical perspective on their practice with their immigrant students, especially in the context of the struggles, both emotional and financial, that these individuals face.

ROBERT PINET

Acknowledgment

The author thanks Brian Morgan for reading and providing valuable commentary on earlier versions of this work, as well as the two anonymous readers who reviewed the manuscript for the *TESL Canadd Journal*.

The Author

Robert Pinet teaches ESL writing courses at Humber College in Toronto and is a doctoral student in Curriculum, Teaching and Learning/Comparative, International and Development Education at the Ontario Institute for Studies in Education of the University of Toronto.

References

Bettencourt, E. (2003). LINC then and now: 10-year anniversary. *Contact, 29*(2), 25-28.

Bobbitt, F. (1924). *How to make a curriculum*. Boston, MA: Houghton Mifflin.

Bullard, J. (1989). Citizenship education: A trivial pursuit? *TESL Talk, 19*(1), 19-28.

Centre for Language Training and Assessment 9CLTA). (2004). *Guidelines for LINC assessment centres in Ontario*. Mississauga, ON: Author.

Cleghorn, L. (2000). *Valuing English: An ethnography of a federal language training program for adult immigrants*. Unpublished master's thesis, University of Toronto.

Cray, E. (1997). Teachers' perceptions of a language policy: "Teaching LINC." *TESL Canada Journal, 15*(1), 22-37.

Derwing, T.M. (1992). Instilling a passive voice: Citizenship instruction in Canada. In B. Burnaby & A. Cumming (Eds.), *Socio-political aspects of ESL* (pp. 193-202). Toronto, ON: OISE Press.

Derwing, T.M., & Munro, M. (1987). Citizenship preparation in Canada: An overview. *TESL Talk, 19*(1), 35-41.

Dewey, J. (1897). My pedagogical creed. *School Journal, 44*(3), 77-80. [Electronic version]. Retrieved September 24, 2005, from: http://www.infed.org/archives/e-texts/e-dew-pc.htm

Dewey, J. (1931). *The way out of educational confusion* (the Inglish Lecture). Wesport, CT: Greenwood Press.

Fox, J., & Courchêne, R. (2005). The Canadian Language Benchmarks (CLB): A critical appraisal. *Contact, 31*(2), 5-26.

Freire, P. (2001). *Pedagogy of the oppressed* (30th anniversary edition). New York: Continuum.

Giroux, H. (1983). Critical theory and rationality in citizenship education. In H. Giroux & D. Purpel (Eds.), *The hidden curriculum and moral education: Deception or discovery?* (pp. 321-360) Berkeley, CA: McCutchan.

Maslow, A. (1970). *Motivation and personality*. New York: Harper & Row.

Maslow, A. (1971). *The farther reaches of human nature*. New York: Viking.

Miller, J.P., & Seller, W. (1990). *Curriculum: Perspectives and practice*. Toronto, ON: Copp Clark Pitman.

Morgan, B. (1995/1996). Promoting and assessing critical language awareness. *TESOL Journal, 2*(2), 13-17.

Pawlikoswka-Smith, G. (2000). *Canadian language benchmarks 2000: English as a second language—For adults*. Ottawa, ON: Citizenship and Immigration Canada.

Richardson, A.S. (1999). *Ideologically speaking: Teacher conversations about practice in relation to the program mandate for LINC, Language Instruction for Newcomers to Canada*. Unpublished master's thesis, Simon Fraser University.

Rogers, C. (1969). *Freedom to learn*. Columbus, OH: Merrill.

Sears, A.M., & Hughes, A.S. (1996). Citizenship education and current educational reform. *Canadian Journal of Education, 21*(2), 123-142.

Schwab, J. (1973). The practical: Translation into curriculum. *School Review*, August, 501-522.

Thomson, R., & Derwing, T.M. (2004). Presenting Canadian values in LINC: The role of textbooks and teachers. *TESL Canada Journal 21*(2), 17-33.

Toronto Catholic District School Board (TCDSB). (1999). *The LINC 4 & 5 curriculum guidelines: A computer-integrated curriculum based on Canadian language benchmarks 4-6.* Toronto, ON: Author.

Wilber, K. (1983). *A sociable god.* New York: McGraw-Hill.

Witol, P. (2004). Incorporating competency-based Canadian Language Benchmarks into a theme-based curriculum. *Contact, 30*(2), 15-22.

"I Meant to Say That": How Adult Language Learners Construct Positive Identities Through Nonstandard Language Use

Michelle Szabo

The aim of this article is to raise awareness in L2 education about the relationship between second-language learners' linguistic choices in the L2 and their identities. The author reviews empirical research and language-learning narratives that show that L2 learners may purposely use nonstandard L2 forms. Using a poststructuralist framework to conceptualize identity, the author argues that these second-language learners use nonstandard language in the L2 in order to create positive identities, and in some cases to resist social inequalities, in the L2 community. The implications of this research for second-language teachers are discussed and suggestions for classroom practice are offered.

Cet article a comme objectif de conscientiser le milieu d'enseignement en langue seconde quant au rapport entre les choix linguistiques que font les apprenants dans leur L2, d'une part, et leur identité, d'autre part. L'auteure passe en revue des récits portant sur l'apprentissage d'une L2 et des recherches empiriques qui indiquent que les apprenants en L2 choisissent parfois d'employer des formes non standard ou populaires dans leur L2. S'appuyant sur un cadre poststructuraliste pour concepter l'identité, l'auteure fait valoir son point de vue selon lequel les apprenants de L2 emploient un langage populaire dans leur L2 pour se créer, au sein de la communauté de langue seconde, une identité positive et, dans certains cas, résister à des inégalités sociales. L'article se termine par une discussion des conséquences de cette recherche pour les enseignants en langue seconde et la présentation de suggestions pour la pratique en salle de classe.

Introduction: Error Correction and Additional Language-Learner Identity

Additional language (AL)[1] instructors are often faced with the task of identifying and correcting learners' errors. Considerable attention has been paid in pedagogical research and teacher education to when and how teachers should give error feedback to learners (Chaudron, 1977; Lightbown & Spada, 1990; Lyster & Ranta, 1997). However, this focus on timing and method, although valuable, may not be enough to help AL teachers fully deal with the complex endeavor of error correction. The question of what kinds of utterances should be corrected in the first place also merits our attention.

Language instructors whose students wish to improve in several areas of communicative competence (Canale & Swain, 1980) may be concerned not only about errors of form, but also about sociolinguistic and pragmatic errors. They may endeavor not only to help learners be intelligible in the AL, but also to communicate in ways that seem appropriate to their interlocutors. In other words, these teachers may correct utterances that seem inappropriate considering factors such as learners' age or sex, the context of interaction, and cultural norms, thinking that such corrections will help learners to give positive impressions of themselves in the AL. Teachers who are concerned about discrimination based on nonnative accent may also attempt to correct intelligible but "accented" pronunciation.

Indeed, helping learners to create positive impressions of themselves in the AL—which may involve helping them to approximate the standard dialect—is an important responsibility of AL instructors. However, I suggest here that correcting nonstandard utterances of AL learners may also in certain cases be damaging to learners' identities. A number of empirical studies and personal narratives, to which I turn below, show that learners do not in all cases wish to emulate native speakers of the standard AL. In fact, this research indicates that AL learners may purposely reject certain AL variants.[2]

There has been increasing interest in the relationship between additional language and identity in applied linguistics research (*Journal of Language, Identity and Education*, 2003-present; *TESOL Quarterly, 31*[3], 1997; *TESOL Quarterly, 33*[3], 1999; *Linguistics and Education, 8*[1],(2), 1996; *International Journal of Bilingualism, 5*[3], 2001; Norton, 2000). However, the research has mainly focused on how multilinguals construct desired identities in certain contexts by using one of their languages instead of another (Blackledge & Pavlenko, 2001; Pavlenko & Piller, 2001). It has also focused on how language learners resist social inequalities in the AL community by using their native language when the AL is called for (Heller, 1996; Lin, 2000; Miller, 2000) or by claiming their right to be heard in the AL despite their "nonnative" status (Norton Peirce, 1995; Pavlenko, 2001). There has been little consideration of how AL learners may negotiate their identities through the purposeful rejection of standard AL forms. Although a small number of studies have investigated this subject (which I discuss in detail below), I have seen little attention to the relationship between identity and choice of AL forms by language learners in literature for AL educators. This article aims to bring the trends in this research and their pedagogical implications to the attention of AL instructors.

Focus: A Subset of AL Learners

In this article, I focus on teenage and adult AL learners as opposed to child AL learners or proficient bilinguals or multilinguals. My focus on teenagers and adults stems from my interest in the conflicts of identity that may arise for individuals who are learning an AL later in their lives: those whose primary languages[3] (native or first language) have already had a significant influence.

I also limit the current investigation to learners who do not see themselves as belonging to a social group whose members use an indigenized variety of English (such as Indian English, Singapore English, and Filipino English). A thorough discussion of why language educators and researchers concerned with indigenized varieties of English should steer away from native-speaker models is provided elsewhere (Sridhar & Sridhar, 1994).

Theoretical Framework

Identity Defined

Borrowing Weedon's (1997) definition, I take *identity* to mean "[the individual's] sense of herself and her ways of understanding her relation to the world" (p. 32). Various scholars have defined identity more precisely in terms of social group membership (Giles & Johnson, 1981; Pavlenko, 2001; Tajfel, 1974). Social group membership is indeed one important element of an individual's identity; however, I believe that learners' use of an AL is related not only to their sense of themselves as members of socially recognizable groups such as Canadians, women, Blacks, and so forth, but also to their sense of themselves as *individuals* with characteristics such as *polite, competent Japanese speaker*, and *mature*. Therefore, I use Weedon's definition of identity, taking it to mean both an individual's sense of membership in a particular social group and what Ting-Toomey (1999) called "personal identity," an individual's sense of himself or herself as a unique individual.

Identity and Language

Although a number of theories attempt to explain the relationship between identity and language (e.g., variationist sociolinguistics, the social psychological paradigm, among others), poststructuralist theories seem to be the most useful in understanding the relationship between AL learners' identities and the AL variants that they use. For poststructuralists, identity is not something that people have, but something that people construct through their behavior and, more specifically, through their language (Butler, 1990; Weedon, 1997). The premise is that identity is fluid and is always in the process of being formed (Weedon). Every time individuals speak, their use of particular linguistic variants shapes how others see them and how they see themselves.

If language is the site of identity construction, then identity must also be context-dependent and multiple (Norton Peirce, 1995). From this point of view, people expose and create different aspects of their identities in different situations. Moreover, because identity is multiple, it is also contradictory, because some aspects of a person's identity may conflict with others (Butler, 1990; Weedon, 1997). Identity is also taken to be a "site of struggle" (Norton Peirce) because individuals continually attempt to define themselves while social discourses continually redefine them (Blackledge & Pavlenko, 2001).

In this article, I write under the assumption that identity is constructed in language, and that it is flexible, multiple, and a site of struggle.

The Importance of Standard and Native-Like Language

As suggested above, AL learners do not necessarily wish to use only standard, native-like variants in the AL. Some learners may in certain situations reject particular standard variants in favour of variants of a nondominant AL dialect (e.g., an ethnic or regional variety) or variants of their primary language (PL). However, this is not to say that learners should not learn and be taught the standard dialect or that instructors should allow all instances of transfer from the PL. On the contrary, it is vital that learners become familiar with the standard AL dialect.

There are several reasons for this. Immigrants or learners temporarily in an AL community know that speaking "like a native" may enhance their abilities to build personal relationships with other AL speakers.[4] Numerous studies show that both native and nonnative speakers may have unfavourable opinions of AL learners who make sociolinguistic or pragmatic errors or have nonnative accents (Fayer & Krasinski, 1987, Lindemann, 2002; Munro, 2003; Pavlenko, 2001). For learners in an AL community, these personal relationships may be necessary not only for emotional well-being, but also for access to the material resources that they need to succeed in the new country (Norton, 2000). Although using the AL "like a native" may not be a priority for AL learners who do not wish to live in an AL community—those who are learning an AL for international communication, for example—being intelligible is. These learners know that using too many variants from their PL in an AL is likely to reduce their intelligibility. Finally, adult AL learners, whether learning an AL as a foreign, second, or international language, are aware that learning a standard AL dialect is beneficial because of its "symbolic capital" (Bourdieu, 1991) or its "ability to provide access to more prestigious forms of education and desired positions in the workforce or on the social mobility ladder" (Pavlenko, 2002, p. 283).

MICHELLE SZABO

The Negotiation of Adult AL Learner Identities Through AL Variants: Findings of Empirical Studies and Personal Narratives

Although there are several benefits to using standard AL variants and the use of nonstandard variants is often stigmatized, the studies that I consider below show that AL learners may consciously use nonstandard AL variants. As a group, these studies suggest that AL learners may purposely use nonstandard variants because these variants help them to create what to them are positive identities in the AL. I use the term *positive* rather than *ideal* because AL learners may be limited in terms of the identities that they are able to choose. We see that because AL learners are faced with conflicting social discourses from at least two languages (the AL and PL), various aspects of their identities come to be in conflict. We also see that because of these conflicts, learners may wish to choose nonstandard variants, but choose standard variants.

Transfer of PL Variants to an AL

The following studies show that some AL learners purposely transfer variants from their PL into the AL.[5] It seems that these learners feel more comfortable—or more "like themselves"—in some cases using PL variants than they would if they used AL variants. In some situations, learners may even use PL variants in the AL as a way of resisting what they perceive as social inequalities in the AL community.

Vocal, lexical, and pragmatic variants. A study by Ohara (2000) shows that some United States women learning Japanese used pitch to negotiate their identities in Japan. More specifically, these women constructed positive identities for themselves in Japanese by using a lower pitch than is expected of them as female speakers. A detailed look at Ohara's study offers insight into the relationship between pitch and identity in Japan.

Ohara's (2000) study was motivated by earlier studies that revealed that some Japanese women fluent in English used higher voice pitch in Japanese than in English. The author argues that this is because in Japanese, a high-pitched voice connotes a variety of characteristics associated with Japanese femininity such as cuteness, weakness, and politeness. Ohara's study was an attempt to see whether the opposite is also the case—whether English-speaking learners of Japanese "employ a higher pitch when speaking Japanese in order to satisfy cultural expectations" (p. 234).

To answer this question, the researcher interviewed and recorded the voices of 10 female Japanese learners with English as their PL in a variety of English and Japanese speaking tasks. Five were beginning learners who had never lived in Japan and the other five were advanced learners who had lived at least one year in Japan. She found that among the five learners who were aware of the social significance of pitch in Japan, only three used a higher pitch in Japanese than in English.

Ohara (2000) turns to her interview data to explain these results. The two women who did not raise their pitch in Japanese both stressed that despite wanting to be accepted by Japanese people, they did not feel comfortable raising their pitch. One woman claimed that this was because to her, using a high-pitched voice was unnatural and fake and she wanted to "use her natural voice" (pp. 244-245). The other emphasized that for her, the use of high pitch by Japanese women made them seem immature. These learners carefully considered the impression that their use of a high pitch would give to others. It seems that this impression—as "fake woman" or "immature woman"—was not consistent with the identities that they wished to construct in Japanese.

For one of the learners in this study (Ohara, 2000), refusing to use the pitch expected of her in Japan was a way of creating a positive identity, but also a way of resisting gender inequalities that she saw in Japan. This learner said that she purposely did not use a high pitch in Japanese because she believed that the use of a high pitch by Japanese women contributed to their oppression by Japanese men. She explained:

> I feel bad for Japanese women because men treat them so poorly sometimes, and I can understand how it would be so difficult for them to break out of their traditional roles. But even so, I think by willingly taking on such a cute way of acting and using language they contribute very much to being treated that way. (p. 246)

For this woman, resisting gender inequality in Japan meant using a nonstandard pitch in Japanese.

The three women who did raise their pitch in Japanese also mentioned a resistance to doing so. But for them, the desire to be accepted by Japanese people outweighed their negative feelings about using a high pitch. One of the three clearly expressed that her use of a high pitch despite her aversion to it, was fueled by a desire to use appropriate Japanese: "It's not like I enjoy talking in a high pitched voice but it's like you kind of have to do that when speaking in Japanese" (Ohara, 2000, p. 243).

The feelings of these learners remind us of the conflict that AL learners may feel when learning a language with a different social organization than their PL. The desire to be accepted by Japanese people and to speak correct Japanese was a strong motivation for these women to use a high pitch. On the other hand, their desire to create identities that were acceptable to them and to feel equal to Japanese men encouraged them to use a low pitch.

Research by Siegal (1994, 1995, 1996) on Western women learning Japanese complements Ohara's (2000) findings. Like Ohara, Siegal demonstrates that some Western women learning Japanese resisted inequality and created positive identities for themselves by using nonstandard variants in Japanese, including nonstandard pitch. But Siegal's informants did this also by avoiding particles and exclamations associated with Japanese women's language.

During her ethnographic research of four white Western women learning Japanese in Japan, Siegal (1994) found that two of the women—who each had intermediate to advanced Japanese proficiency—purposely avoided some elements of Japanese language. Arina, a 25-year-old native Hungarian speaker, explained her dislike of humble Japanese women's language when referring to a female Japanese acquaintance: "I cannot stand the way she talks. She is so humble all the time. I don't want to be that humble. I am just going to stick with the [polite form], it is polite and safe" (p. 647). Whereas she saw Japanese women's language as redundant, she thought Japanese men's language was "direct and clean" (p. 647). This is perhaps why she avoided the prefix *o*, associated with Japanese women's language, even after being chastised for doing so by a Japanese male acquaintance.

The other woman in Siegal's (1994) ethnographic research who showed resistance to Japanese women's language was Sally, a 21-year-old Western woman. She expressed her dislike of the high-pitched voice, enthusiastic demeanor and exclamations (*sugoi ne!* [that's great!], *kirei ne!* [that's beautiful!]) associated with young Japanese women's language. For her, these elements of the speech of young Japanese women seemed "babyish," "irritating," and "unnatural" (p. 645). Although she admitted that this language was perhaps natural for young Japanese women, she mentioned trying but not being able to continue to use this language herself. She seemed particularly troubled by her observation that some young women were "not saying anything deep or meaningful about [the subject]" (p. 645) and that they changed their demeanor and language around men. Although Sally and Arina did not express feeling a conflict between using Japanese appropriately and using language that suited their identities, Sally did mention to Siegal that a friend of hers had such a concern. When Sally asked her friend why she used what to Sally seemed silly and childish women's expressions and demeanor, her friend replied that "she didn't like it either but she felt that she had to ... it's what's expected of you" (p. 645).

Ogulnick (1998), a US applied linguist, describes a similar experience to that of the participants in Ohara's (2000) and Siegal's (1994, 1995, 1996) work in her personal account of learning Japanese in Japan. She expresses her initial desire "to fit into the culture as much as possible," which led her to use variants (e.g., low volume, high pitch, tentativeness) that she was uncomfortable using but that were expected of her. The conflict between her desire to fit in and her desire to maintain an identity as a strong woman is obvious: "My desire to be accepted and recognized as a speaker of Japanese overpowered any subconscious resistance I may have had to complying with what I perceived as submissive behaviour" (p. 135). However, she also describes how her feelings changed over time as she gained more experience interacting in Japanese. At a later point in her stay in Japan, she resisted using standard variants despite her desire to be accepted in Japan because she saw these variants as contributing to gender inequality and her own possible oppression by Japanese men. She describes her feelings:

[I had a] strong internal sense … when I first went to Japan to find my place among a group of women, even if it meant having to change the way I looked, acted and spoke. Conversely, I became more resistant to speaking "like a woman," or *kirei na nihongo* [pretty Japanese] when I sensed that, by doing so, I was submitting to patriarchal control. (p. 105)

Like the participants in Ohara's and Siegal's work, Ogulnick negotiated an identity in Japanese by using standard and nonstandard variants.

In her autobiographical reflection on language and culture, Mori (1997), a Japanese woman who emigrated to the US in her 20s, expresses similar feelings about Japanese to those expressed by the women mentioned above. The conflict between using appropriate language and language that reflects one's identity is obvious in her words.

Every word I say [in Japanese] forces me to be elaborately polite, indirect, submissive, and unassertive. There is no way I can sound intelligent, clearheaded, or decisive. But if I did not speak a "proper" feminine language, I would sound stupid in another way—like someone who is uneducated, insensitive, and rude, and therefore cannot be taken seriously. (p. 12)

Although Mori is a native Japanese speaker (and not an AL learner of Japanese), her perspective adds to our understanding of women's feelings about Japanese forms.

Millison (2000), in a personal narrative about his experience as an American learning Mandarin, living in China, and interacting with Chinese in-laws, also writes about his uneasiness when using some of the standard variants in his AL. Like the women discussed above, he felt a clash between his identity and ways of speaking that were expected of him by the AL community. He articulates his resistance to the hierarchy and indirectness in the pragmatic conventions of this language: "Evasion, submission, and yielding still grate against my sense of myself as an outspoken American who says what he means in a culture that values emotional transparence [sic] and openness" (p. 150). Kasper and Zhang (1995) report a similar case of an American woman learning Mandarin who found Mandarin address terms for adult women offensive.

The female Japanese and Mandarin learners discussed here were uneasy using standard variants that they felt positioned them as tentative and in-ferior because of their sex, and the male Mandarin learner felt conflicted using Mandarin variants that to him positioned him as tentative and inferior because of his age and his status vis-à-vis his in-laws.[6]

Phonological variants. A study by Gatbonton (1975, as cited in Dowd, Zuengler, & Berkowitz, 1990) reveals the possibility that some French-speaking Canadian learners of English may transfer phonological variants from French into English for reasons related to their identities. Looking at the English development of both "nationalistic" (having strong pro-French attitudes) and "non-nationalistic" (having strong pro-English attitudes) learners, she found "a significantly higher development for both /__/ and /__/ among the *non*-nationalistic learners" (p. 19, emphasis in original). Although there are a number of reasons not related to identity for which this might be the case (e.g., non-nationalistic learners have more contact with English speakers and/or more exposure to English materials), it is possible that nationalistic learners deliberately used nonstandard pronunciation. This argument, although speculative, is not unreasonable given Gatbonton's findings about the attitudes of *listeners* toward French-accented English speech. As revealed in a later report on Gatbonton's results, "the non[French]-accented speakers (and in most cases the moderately [French]-accented speakers as well) were judged to be significantly more pro-Anglophone and less pro-Francophone than the heavily [French]-accented speakers" (Gatbonton, Trofimovich, & Magid, in press). It is possible that French-speaking Canadian nationalistic learners of English, knowing about the perceptions of others about French accent and nationalism, purposely avoided standard pronunciation and transferred French phonological variants into their English speech to project a pro-French identity. This would make sense considering that the research was done in the 1970s, a time when there was a threat to the French language in Quebec and an obvious tension between Anglophones and Francophones. It is also possible, as Gatbonton et al. (in press) suggest, that these AL learners did not consciously transfer PL variants into the AL, but strove to improve their English pronunciation only enough to be intelligible. In other words, these English learners may not have seen the point of aiming for native-like pronunciation when "the only 'reward' for doing so [was] aspersions on their group loyalty."

Abercrombie (1949) tells a few interesting anecdotes that also reveal that some learners deliberately transfer phonological variants from their PL to the AL. The daughters of one of his colleagues, who had been educated in France, admitted that they used English-accented French in their British schools because "life at school would be intolerable if they were to use in class the kind of French they used in France" (p. 119). Abercrombie also mentions a conversation that he had with some Egyptian students of English who preferred not to use the British vowel sounds that they had been taught in class. They said that they did not want their friends to hear them speaking in what to them was an affected way.

Surveys have also shown that some AL learners prefer to maintain an accent from their PL in an AL. Benson (1991) asked 311 freshmen at a Japanese university, "Which kind of English would you like to be able to speak well?" He found that although 47.3% chose American English, 24.1% of students preferred "English with a Japanese accent" (p. 41). A survey by Porter and Garvin (1989, cited in Jenkins, 2000) also showed that some learners of English preferred to maintain their (PL) accents rather than adopting native-like pronunciation.

In this section, I examine empirical studies and language learning narratives that suggest that learners of Japanese, Mandarin, and English may use nonstandard variants in the AL. Work by Ohara (2000), Siegal (1994, 1995, 1996), Ogulnick (1998), Millison (2000), and Kasper and Zhang (1995) suggests that Western learners of some Asian languages may be uncomfortable using standard variants in these languages because they feel that these variants position them as inferior, weak, or indecisive. These learners may transfer variants of pitch, register, and pragmatics from their PL into the AL or simply avoid AL variants such as gendered particles or address terms. The data also reveal that although some Western learners may be uncomfortable using standard Asian variants, they may do so anyway because of their desire to be accepted and gain social (and perhaps material) benefits in the AL community.

The work of Gatbonton (1975), Gatbonton et al. (in press), Abercrombie (1949), Benson (1991), and Porter and Garvin (1989) suggests that AL learners may wish to keep their PL accents as a signal to listeners of their linguistic background, political leanings, or group solidarity. These studies reveal that learners of English may transfer phonological variants from their PL (French, Arabic, Japanese) into the AL.

Variants of a Recognized Nondominant Dialect

The studies in this section, like those above, reveal that some AL learners consciously use nonstandard variants to construct positive identities in the AL. In the following studies, learners do not transfer variants from their PL, however, but use variants of a nondominant dialect.

Ibrahim (1999) shows that Black English (BE) may be a linguistic target for some English learners in North America. After a six-month ethnographic study of 16 Black immigrant youths from Africa at an urban Canadian high school, he concluded that some of his participants used BE as a way of constructing positive racial identities in their new environment.

More specifically, Ibrahim (1999) found that many of his male informants were attempting to learn and use Black Stylized English (BSE), a subcategory of BE. These youths tended to use grammatical variants typical of BE such as distributive *be* and negative concord, which they learned from African-American rap and hip-hop music. He suggests that they chose to adopt this English dialect because they saw themselves "mirrored" in African-

MICHELLE SZABO

American pop culture. According to those who used BSE, they identified with the purveyors of African-American pop culture because of genetic connections and because they shared similar racist and race-mediated experiences. One BSE user suggested that a Black person using standard English would be as strange as a Black person playing country music.

Especially interesting about this study is that the learners who decided to use variants of BE to signal their Blackness did not identify themselves as Black before arriving in Canada. Ibrahim (1999), himself an immigrant from Africa, explains that in Sudan his Blackness was not a salient aspect of his identity. It was only when he arrived in Canada that his race was highlighted—as he was positioned as Black by others—and he developed an identity as Black. Ibrahim sees his research participants as experiencing the same shifts in identity in the North American social world. For him these youths make a place for themselves in Canada by "becoming Black" (p. 354). They create an identity that North Americans understand by using BE variants.

We can see that these youths are limited in terms of the ethnic identities they can construct in Canada. Although many of the youths were from Somalia, they could not, for example, construct identities as Somali, because Somali is not a widely recognized identity in Canada that can be signalled through English variants. Pavlenko (2001), in her investigation of the autobiographies of bilingual writers in the US, found that some of the authors who were immigrants to the US encountered the same limitations. She notes,

> Many authors ... suggest that certain ethnic identities may be hard or even impossible to perform in the U.S.A. context. Thus new arrivals may face the fact that their own identity categories are meaningless to the members of their new community and that they have to reposition themselves (or to allow others to reposition them) in order to be "meaningful" in the new environment. (p. 331)

So the teenaged boys used BE to construct positive, though not ideal identities. In North America, they recognized that they were positioned as Black by others. Instead of resisting this positioning, Ibrahim argues, they took pride in these identities and strengthened them by choosing BE variants. In this way, they collaborated with the mainstream by positioning themselves as Black, but at the same time resisted social inequalities by celebrating Blackness (Ibrahim, 1999).

Ibrahim's (1999) study also shows that the identities available to the young African women were more limited than those available to the young men. He notes that although the younger African girls in his ethnography used some variants of BE, the older girls used mainly variants of plain Canadian English (the dominant dialect). He proposes that this was because the hip-hop and rap music from which the boys learned BE and with which BE is associated often contains sexist language. Although the girls may have wished to create positive identities as Black, they may have found that they were not able to do so without compromising their identities as respectable young women. They were limited in their ability to construct both positive racial and gender identities.

An earlier study by Goldstein (1987) also shows that AL learners may use variants of a nondominant dialect. Like the learners in Ibrahim's (1999) study, Goldstein's participants used variants of BE, but unlike Ibrahim's participants, they were not Black. The participants in Goldstein's study were all Latin Americans with Spanish as their PL.

Goldstein's (1987) participants were 28 teenage males who were learning English. The purpose of the study was to find out why those who used BE variants did so. The researcher used statistical methods to find the relationship between learners' use of two BE variants (negative concord and distributive *be*) and first, "extent of contact with Black Americans," and second, "feelings of identification with Black Americans" (p. 421). Extent of contact and feelings of identification were determined through a multiple-choice questionnaire.

Goldstein (1987) reports that although there was a significant correlation between *extent of contact with Black Americans* and BE, there was no correlation between the learners' identification with Blacks and their use of BE. Although the researcher proposes that this unexpected result may have come from faulty methodology or an inaccurate measurement of *identification with Black Americans*, I would argue that it may in fact be accurate. Her participants may have used BE for reasons related to their identities, but not as Blacks. One idea is that they used BE to signal their "coolness." Reporting on a comparable study of children aged 11-13, Poplack (1978) argues that Puerto Rican learners of English who had almost no contact with Black Americans used BE because of its "covert prestige" (p. 101). Similarly, Cutler (1999) argues that the White teenager in her ethnography used BE as a symbol not of Blackness, but of a commodified ("hip") lifestyle. Another idea is that Goldstein's participants may have used BE as a way of distancing themselves from mainstream (white) culture, but at the same time, avoiding the stigma of sounding like nonnative speakers. They may have used BE to construct positive identities from among those available to them in English. Whatever the reasons, it is clear that the learners in Goldstein's study chose Black English over the standard dialect.

The studies in this section suggest that AL learners may project positive identities for themselves by using variants of a nondominant AL dialect. Research by Ibrahim (1999) and Goldstein (1987) reveals that some African and Hispanic learners of English learned and used Black English as a way of constructing "Black" and perhaps, "hip" or "nonwhite" identities. As I propose in the above section, although these English learners may not have

MICHELLE SZABO

been able to construct ideal identities in the AL, they constructed positive identities with the resources that were available to them.

Contexts of AL Use and Consequences of Variant Choices

We see that AL learners may make AL variant choices based on how particular variants affect their identities. However, it is important to note that AL learners are not always free to make such choices. The material or social consequences of using particular variants—regardless of how these variants affect learners' identities—may leave learners no choice but to avoid them.

As mentioned above, immigrants and sojourners in AL countries may find that the material and social benefits of using standard and native-like AL variants far outweigh the potential gains to their identities of using nonstandard language. Research on public attitudes in Canada, the US, and Australia has shown that some residents of these three countries are intolerant toward those with noticeable PL influences in their AL (Tse, 2001; Cummins, 1990; Miller, 2000). In fact, in interviews with 100 adult immigrant AL learners in Edmonton, Derwing (2003) found that although there were accounts of acceptance and patience, there were many more accounts of discrimination or rudeness that were thought to be related to learners' accented English. This intolerance may be why 95% of the learners in this study stated that they wished to develop native-like English pronunciation. It could also be because these learners were able to continue interacting in their PL and saw it, not English, as a medium to express their ethnic identities.

However, not all countries are generally intolerant toward deviations from standard or native-like language. Some of the learners in Ohara's (2000) study mentioned that they were "allowed" to resist Japanese norms. One women was told by her host mother that because she was a foreigner, she was not expected to speak in a feminine way. Another noted that despite using her "natural voice" in Japanese, she "was able to make many very good Japanese friends" (p. 245). Scholars interested in Japan (Siegal, 1996; Loveday, 1982) have also expressed the idea that Japanese people have low expectations of the Japanese proficiency of Caucasians. Had these women been ostracized in their host society for using their normal pitch, they might have decided to raise it.

On the other hand, some female AL learners have had more to worry about in choosing AL variants than being understood and accepted. Sexual harassment and aggression has had an influence on the variants that some women have chosen. Ohara (2000) mentions that one of the three women in her study who generally raised her pitch in Japanese did not necessarily do so in all contexts. The learner explained:

At some *enkai* [parties] when some of the older men employees would get drunk and try to act a little too friendly, I made sure I changed my mannerisms and actions so they would know I didn't like that kind of stuff ... I was not conscious of lowering the pitch of my voice, but I am sure I did that too. (p. 246)

Had this learner used standard variants in this situation, she might have encouraged her male interlocutors in their mistreatment of her. One of Siegal's (1994) participants, Sally, was also the victim of sexual harassment. This may have been one reason why she had negative feelings about variants of Japanese women's language that to her seemed childish or passive. Ehrlich's (2000) overview of studies that document the sexual harassment or abuse of female AL learners indicates clearly that such experiences are not uncommon.

Because of the consequences of particular AL variant choices in varying contexts, identity negotiation may be a secondary concern for some AL learners. Social acceptance and safety may encourage AL learners in certain contexts to choose particular variants instead of others.

Implications for AL Education

I show that AL learners may purposely use nonstandard variants in an AL, either variants from their PL or from a nondominant dialect. I also argue that AL learners may use nonstandard variants in particular situations because in so doing they may construct positive identities or resist being positioned as unequal in the AL community. These findings have a number of implications for AL education.

Nonstandard Variants Are Not Necessarily Mistakes

First, AL teachers should keep in mind (and perhaps discuss with their students) that standard variants are not linguistically superior to non-dominant variants, but have achieved or been assigned a higher status because of their use by powerful social groups (Milroy & Milroy, 1991). Smitherman and Cunningham (1997) propose that regular classroom teachers help their African-American students understand that Black English is not *bad* English by discussing in class the history of English dialects and the sociopolitical factors influencing their relative prestige. AL teachers whose students may be interested in (or misinformed about) nondominant dialects may find it useful to do something similar in their AL classrooms.

Second, AL teachers should be aware that what may seem like a mistake may in fact be a learner's deliberate expression of her or his identity. This is not to say that teachers should stop correcting mistakes. Nor am I suggesting that language instructors ought to know the difference between purposeful and unintentional mistakes. I am simply suggesting that teachers be open to the possibility of resistance to the standard. Of course, if an AL learner is unintelligible, correction is necessary. But because we are speaking here of

MICHELLE SZABO

variants—linguistic forms with the same literal meanings—the substitution of one variant for another should not affect learners' intelligibility.[7]

On the other hand, it is important to remember that learners' use of nonstandard variants may be misinterpreted by listeners. Listeners may misjudge AL learners (as rude, childish, or uneducated, for example) if these learners use variants that are not expected of them in certain contexts and as (perceived) members of particular social groups (Gumperz, 1982). Therefore, teachers should explore with learners possible interpretations of relevant nonstandard variants.

AL Learners May Negotiate Their Identities Through Nonstandard Variants

AL educators who are interested in helping learners build positive identities in the AL may wish to encourage students to express any negative feelings they may have about particular AL variants. Following Norton Peirce (1995), I would suggest that such teachers encourage learners to keep diaries of their AL interactions, noting surprising occurrences or others that made them uncomfortable. Teachers can collect these diaries periodically and use students' observations to structure future class discussions. During such discussions, teachers can help learners to discover the social meanings and consequences of using particular standard and nonstandard variants in the AL community. Another idea would be for teachers to use learners' diaries to create scenarios in which learners have to imagine themselves and decide what they would say and how. Teachers may, for example, have learners consider an interaction between an AL speaker and an AL learner in which one or the other was made to feel uncomfortable and then discuss what might have caused the problem (Dunnett, Dubin, & Lezberg, 1986).

Code-Switching Can Be a Useful Tool for Learners

AL teachers and learners should consider the benefits of code-switching—using either standard or nonstandard variants of a particular linguistic unit (e.g., high or low pitch, *am* or *be* as in *I am going* or *I be going*) according to the context of interaction. Smitherman and Cunningham (1997) recommend that Black students (with English as a PL) be encouraged to code-switch between Black English and Standard English using one or the other depending on the context of interaction. I would suggest that AL learners could also benefit from learning to code-switch. They may code-switch between PL variants and native variants or between variants of the dominant dialect and variants of a nondominant dialect depending on the context of interaction and the social and economic consequences of using one or the other. Some AL learners, like the young Hispanic learners in Goldstein's (1987) study, may even learn to code-switch on their own.

Power is Created and Reproduced in Language

As shown above, AL learners may feel that social inequalities are reflected in particular AL variants. But what do we do with this information if we as AL speakers and AL teachers do not see such inequalities ourselves? We may suppose that AL learners perceive inequalities where they do not exist because of being biased by their PL cultures. On the other hand, it is important to consider that AL learners may have special insights into power relations reproduced in language that are invisible to AL speakers.[8] Although this is a complex matter and may not be easily dealt with in the classroom, AL teachers should keep in mind that power is created and reproduced in language. As Norton (2000) notes,

> While it is important for language learners to understand what Hymes (1979) calls the "rules of use" of the target language, it is equally important for them to explore whose interests these rules serve. What is considered appropriate usage is not self-evident (Bourne, 1988), but must be understood with reference to inequitable relations of power between interlocutors. (p.16)

As educators, we should ask ourselves: When we are teaching standard variants, are we in fact teaching some learners how to be oppressed in the AL community? For example, when Japanese educators teach women to use a high pitch or the honorific register in Japanese, are they teaching these women to sound weak and consequently to be weak in Japanese communities? When English teachers teach students that double negatives are incorrect, are they teaching them that African Americans who use Black English are uneducated or unintelligent?

The way to proceed seems to be not to tell learners which variants to use and which not to use, but to show learners their options. Our job as teachers is not to tell learners how to speak in the AL (and thus who to become), but to examine with them their choices and the potential consequences of these choices.

Concluding Remarks

The studies and personal narratives reviewed in this article focus mainly on the experiences and feelings of Western learners of Japanese and Mandarin and African and Hispanic learners of English. Although these learners represent a minute proportion of AL learners worldwide, their experiences are valuable because they raise our awareness of the intricate relationship between identity and AL variants and of the possibility that other AL learners may encounter similar issues. Needless to say, future research in this area that considers learners of other languages and learners with other backgrounds will be a valuable addition to our understanding of AL learning and identity.

MICHELLE SZABO

Notes

[1]In this artilcle, I use the term *additional language (AL)* instead of *second language* or *foreign language*. This is because I consider here language learning in both second-language and foreign-language situations. It is also because I recognize the problematic implications of the term *second language* (discussed elsewhere, see Jenkins, 2000).

[2]I borrow the term *variants* from variationist sociolinguistics, which takes as a premise that there exist in a language different grammatical, lexical, and phonological forms (variants) with the same literal meaning (Chambers, 2002). For example, in English, the words *car* and *automobile* are different lexical variants of the same object. However, whereas variationist sociolinguistics is interested in the different variants that native speakers use in their native language, I use variants to refer to the different linguistic forms with the same literal meaning that adult AL learners use in the AL. I also consider not only grammatical, lexical, and phonological variants, but also pragmatic variants.

[3]I use the term *primary language (PL)* instead of *native language* or *first language* because of the problematic implications of the latter two terms (see Jenkins, 2000, for a detailed discussion of these terms).

[4]I use the term *AL speakers* to mean both native speakers and nonnative speakers of an additional language (AL). My purpose is to emphasize the fact that AL learners, especially learners of international languages, do not interact in the AL only with native speakers, but also with other nonnative speakers.

[5]We see in Siegal (1994, 1995, 1996) that learners may also omit some standard AL variants. I treat this as a transfer from the PL because when learners do not use such variants, they are doing as they would in their PL (English), a language in which gendered particles do not exist.

[6]It is important to note that AL learners interpret the AL and AL culture according to their own perspectives and biases. It is certainly not the case that the Western learners discussed here were more enlightened or wiser than their Asian hosts or that there is necessarily more inequality in Asian than in Western societies. It is also possible that the Western learners in the above studies misinterpreted the social relations expressed in their AL. However, it is important to acknowledge and respect learners' individual feelings about the AL and how it positions them in AL society.

[7]Although this may not be the case for phonological variants, it is also not necessarily the case that nonnative accents lead to misunderstandings (Jenkins, 2002).

[8]I would add that monolingual AL educators may benefit greatly from learning an AL themselves. This experience might give them insights into the inequalities in both the language that they are learning and the one that they teach (see Ogulnick, 1998, for more on learning an AL as a window into the biases of one's own language).

Acknowledgments

I sincerely thank Brian Morgan, whose ideas, enthusiasm, and advice inspired me during the production of various versions of this article. I also thank Lise Szabo, my tireless editor, and the anonymous reviewers of *TESL Canada Journal* for their helpful comments.

The Author

Michelle Szabo is an academic English instructor at the York University English Language Institute in Toronto.

References

Abercrombie, D. (1949). Teaching pronunciation. *English Language Teaching, 3*, 113-122.

Benson, M. (1991). Attitudes and motivation towards English: A survey of Japanese freshmen. *RELC Journal, 1*(2), 34-48.

Blackledge, A., & Pavlenko, A. (2001). Negotiation of identities in multilingual contexts. *International Journal of Bilingualism, 5,* 243-257.

Bourdieu, P. (1991). *Language and symbolic power.* (G. Raymond & M. Adamson, Trans.) Cambridge, MA: Harvard University Press.

Butler, J. (1990). *Gender trouble: Feminism and the subversion of identity.* London: Routledge.

Canale, M., & Swain, M. (1980). Theoretical bases of communicative approaches to second language teaching and testing. *Applied Linguistics, 1*(1), 1-47.

Chambers, J.K. (2002). *Sociolinguistic theory.* Oxford, UK: Blackwell.

Chaudron, C. (1977). A descriptive model of discourse in the corrective treatment of learners' errors. *Language Learning, 27,* 29-46.

Cummins, J. (1990). *Heritage languages: The development and denial of Canada's linguistic resources.* Toronto, ON: Our Schools/Our Selves.

Cutler, C.A. (1999). Yorkville Crossing: White teens, hip hop and African American English. *Journal of Sociolinguistics, 3/4,* 428-442.

Derwing, T. (2003). What do ESL students say about their accents? *Canadian Modern Language Review, 59,* 547-566.

Dowd, J., Zuengler, J., & Berkowitz, D. (1990). L2 social marking: Research issues. *Applied Linguistics, 11*(1), 16-29.

Dunnett, S., Dubin, F., & Lezberg, A. (1986). English language teaching from an intercultural perspective. In J.M. Valdes (Ed.), *Culture bound: Bridging the cultural gap in language teaching* (pp. 148-161). Cambridge, UK: Cambridge University Press.

Ehrlich, S. (2000). Gendering the learner: Sexual harassment and second language acquisition. In A. Pavlenko, A. Blackledge, I. Piller, & M. Teutsch-Dwyer (Eds.), *Multilingualism, second language learning, and gender* (pp. 103-129). Berlin: Mouton de Gruyter.

Fayer, J.M. & Krasinski, E.K. (1987). Native and nonnative judgments of intelligibility and irritation. *Language Learning, 37,* 313-326.

Gatbonton, E., Trofimovich, P., & Magid, M. (in press). Learners' ethnic group affiliation and L2 pronunciation accuracy: A sociolinguistic investigation. *TESOL Quarterly.*

Giles, H., & Johnson, P. (1981). The role of language in ethnic group formation. In J.C. Turner & H. Giles (Eds.), *Intergroup behavior* (pp. 199-243). Oxford, UK: Blackwell.

Goldstein, L.M. (1987). Standard English: The only target for nonnative speakers of English? *TESOL Quarterly, 21,* 417-435.

Gumperz, J. (1982). *Language and social identity.* Cambridge, UK: Cambridge University Press.

Heller, M. (1996). Legitimate language in a multilingual school. *Linguistics and Education, 8,* 139-157.

Ibrahim, A. (1999). Becoming Black: Rap and hip-hop, race, gender, identity, and the politics of ESL learning. *TESOL Quarterly, 33,* 349- 369.

Jenkins, J. (2000). *The phonology of English as an international language.* Oxford, UK: Oxford University Press.

Jenkins, J. (2002). A sociolinguistically-based, empirically-researched pronunciation syllabus for English as an international language. *Applied Linguistics, 23*(1), 83-101.

Kasper, G., & Zhang, Y. (1995). "It's good to be a bit Chinese": Foreign students' experience of Chinese pragmatics. In G. Kasper (Ed.), *Pragmatics of Chinese as a native and target language* (pp. 1-22). Honolulu, HI: University of Hawai'i.

Lightbown, P., & Spada, N. (1990). Focus on form and corrective feedback in communicative language teaching. *Studies in Second Language Acquisition, 12,* 429-448.

Lin, A.M.Y. (2000). Lively children trapped in an island of disadvantage: Verbal play of Cantonese working-class schoolboys in Hong Kong. *International Journal of the Sociology of Language, 143,* 63-83.

Lindemann, S. (2002). Listening with an attitude: A model of native-speaker comprehension of non-native speakers in the United States. *Language in Society, 31*, 419-441.

Loveday, L. (1982). *The sociolinguistics of learning and using a non-native language*. Oxford, UK: Pergamon Press.

Lyster, R., & Ranta, L. (1997). Corrective feedback and learner uptake: Negotiation of form in communicative classrooms. *Studies in Second Language Acquisition, 19*, 37-66.

Miller, J.M. (2000). Language use, identity, and social interaction: Migrant students in Australia. *Research on Language and Social Interaction, 33*(1), 69-100.

Millison, D. (2000). Learning Chinese. In K. Ogulnick (Ed.), *Language crossings* (pp. 143-150). New York: Teachers College Press.

Milroy, J., & Milroy, L. (1991). *Authority in language: Investigating language prescription and standardization*. London: Routledge.

Mori, K. (1997). *Polite lies: On being a woman caught between cultures*. New York: Henry Holt.

Munro, M. (2003). A primer on accent discrimination in the Canadian context. *TESL Canada Journal, 20*(2), 38-51.

Norton, B. (2000). *Identity and language learning: Gender ethnicity and educational change*. London: Pearson Education.

Norton Peirce, B. (1995). Social identity, investment, and language learning. *TESOL Quarterly, 29*(1), 9-31.

Ogulnick, K. (1998). *Onna Rashiku (Like a Woman): The diary of a language learner in Japan*. Albany, NY: SUNY Press.

Ohara, Y. (2000). Finding one's voice in Japanese: A study of pitch levels of L2 users. In A. Pavlenko, A. Blackledge, I. Piller, & M. Teutsch-Dwyer (Eds.), *Multilingualism, second language learning, and gender* (pp. 231-254). Berlin: Mouton de Gruyter.

Pavlenko, A. (2001). "In the world of the tradition, I was unimagined": Negotiation of identities in cross-cultural autobiographies. *International Journal of Bilingualism, 5*, 317-344.

Pavlenko, A. (2002). Poststructuralist approaches to the study of social factors in L2. In V. Cook (Ed.), *Portraits of the L2 user*. Clevedon, UK: Multilingual Matters.

Pavlenko, A., & Piller, I. (2001). New directions in the study of multilingualism, second language learning and gender. In A. Pavlenko, A. Blackledge, I. Piller, & M. Teutsch-Dwyer (Eds.), *Multilingualism, second language learning, and gender* (pp. 17-52). Berlin: Mouton de Gruyter.

Poplack, S. (1978). Dialect acquisition among Puerto Rican bilinguals. *Language and Society, 7*, 89-103.

Siegal, M. (1994). Second-language learning, identity, and resistance: White women studying Japanese in Japan. In M. Bucholz, A. Liang, L. Sutton, & C. Hines (Eds.), *Cultural performances: Proceedings of the third Berkeley Woman and Language conference* (pp. 642-650). Berkeley, CA: Berkeley Woman and Language Group.

Siegal, M. (1995). Individual differences and study abroad: Women learning Japanese in Japan. In B. Freed (Ed.), *Second language acquisition in a study abroad context* (pp. 225-244). Amsterdam: John Benjamins.

Siegal, M. (1996). The role of learner subjectivity in second language sociolinguistic competency: Western women learning Japanese. *Applied Linguistics, 17*, 356-382.

Smitherman, G., & Cunningham, S. (1997). Moving beyond resistance: Ebonics and African American youth. *Journal of Black Psychology, 23*, 227-232.

Sridhar, S.N., & Sridhar, K.K. (1994). Indigenized Englishes as second languages. In R.K. Agnihotri & A.L. Khanna (Eds.), *Second language acquisition* (pp. 41-63). New Delhi: Sage.

Tajfel, H. (1974). Social identity and intergroup behaviour. *Social Science Information, 13*, 65-93.

Ting-Toomey, S. (1999). *Communicating across cultures*. New York: Guilford Press.

Tse, L. (2001). *Why don't they learn English? Separating fact from fallacy in the U.S. language debate*. New York: Teachers College Press.

Weedon, C. (1997). *Feminist practice and poststructuralist theory*. London: Blackwell.

Keeping the Language Focus in Content-Based ESL Instruction Through Proactive Curriculum-Planning

Martha Bigelow, Susan Ranney, and Anne Dahlman

For content-based instruction (CBI) to work to its maximum potential, a concerted planning effort must be made to address language objectives, combined with effective instructional strategies that target and assess student performance in relation to those objectives. In this article, after considering various models of content-language integration, we propose a flexible and dynamic planning model for content-language integration. This model has been helpful in our work with ESL teachers learning to conceptualize lesson planning and curriculum development using CBI across a variety of K-12 settings. Examples implementing the planning model are provided using a curriculum about Arctic exploration and Inuit cultures.

Pour exploiter le plein potentiel de l'enseignement basé sur le contenu (EBC), il faut mettre de l'avant un effort concerté visant les objectifs langagiers ainsi que des stratégies pédagogiques qui ciblent et évaluent la performance des élèves par rapport à ces objectifs. Après avoir étudié divers modèles de planification pour l'intégration contenu-langue, nous en proposons un qui est souple et dynamique. Ce modèle s'est avéré utile lors de notre travail avec des enseignants en ALS qui apprenaient à intégrer la planification de leçons et le développement de programmes d'études s'appuyant sur l'EBC pour divers contextes de la maternelle à la 12ᵉ année. Un programme d'études portant sur l'exploration dans l'Arctique et les cultures inuites sert d'exemple de mise en œuvre du modèle de planification.

Introduction

English as a second language (ESL) teachers in many settings are taking on new roles in their schools that require them to work with academic content. ESL teachers often work alongside content or grade-level teachers to deliver academic content to English language learners (ELLs) in inclusion settings, or they may be using texts and content designed for native speakers in their stand-alone ESL classes. Perhaps they teach their own sheltered-content class or collaborate with a grade level or content teacher in one. This movement toward including content in language instruction helps to meet the crucial need to prepare ELLs for mainstream academic content instruction or include them in mainstream settings (Collier, 1989; Echevarria, Vogt, & Short,

2004; Genesee, 1987; Gibbons, 2002; Snow, Met, & Genesee, 1989). Neverthe-less, the omnipresence of grade-level academic content in the curriculum materials used in ESL can blur the lines between the roles of a content teacher and a language teacher (Pica, 1995). In this article, we argue for the need for ESL teachers to maintain a strong hold on their role as language teachers. To this end, we propose a curriculum-planning model for ensuring the in-clusion of intentional and meaningful language instruction when the ESL teacher is designing language instruction through content. This model presumes that a content theme has already been chosen and offers three points of entry into CBI: the content materials or tasks, the language function, and the linguistic structure, with the point of entry depending on the cir-cumstances of the instruction. The model includes a flexible process of mov-ing between these three points in order to ensure that all are included and closely linked in the curriculum and instruction. The model also includes language learning strategies as a means to move between the three points of the model.

The planning model proposed is inspired by the challenges ESL teachers face when they teach language through content and seeks to offer teachers a tool to aid in their planning for integration. This model is a proposed solu-tion to the common and understandable occurrence that deliberate attention to language (e.g., syntax, pronunciation, vocabulary) is often lost when in-struction shifts its curricular lens away from a language-driven syllabus to a content-based syllabus, a phenomenon that has been recognized in the CBI literature for some time now (Met, 1991; Snow, 2001; Short, 2002; Stoller & Grabe, 1997). Integrating grammar into content may be a new way to teach for many ESL teachers and one in which few have had first-hand experiences as classroom language learners themselves, much less situated mentoring in teaching this way. CBI often calls on teachers to rework their notion of grammar instruction from being an adjunct to content to being closely tied to content (Short). In addition, just as it is difficult for language learners to attend to language and content simultaneously (VanPatten, 1990), it seems difficult for teachers to focus explicitly on content and language in instruc-tion simultaneously. To lessen the cognitive load of this work, we have seen that teachers sometimes devise parallel tracks where traditional grammar is taught alongside thematic content, as in dividing the lesson between the present perfect tense and the content theme. Although the addition of a content component will make the ESL class more engaging, this parallel-track approach fails to bring content and language together because the chosen grammar points do not reflect content-related language, making it difficult for students to apply their study of language to actual uses outside class (Larsen-Freeman, 2001) or to capitalize on connections that may exist with other classes. This parallel approach compartmentalizes bottom-up and top-down language processing, thereby working against the interactive potential CBI affords students.

In order to achieve integration and balance, planning is essential. Met (1991) advocates for planning when she says, "It is inappropriate to assume that desired levels of proficiency and accuracy will emerge miraculously from content lessons taught in a second or foreign language" (p. 285), and Master (2000) concurs by saying, "It is ultimately the CBI instructor who must make sure that grammar is sufficiently covered, both in terms of range and explanation" (p. 102). Proactive planning, however, does not preclude teachers addressing language issues as they arise in a content-based lesson as in giving corrective feedback, but it ensures that language instruction does not totally depend on spontaneous opportunities.

Another by-product of the demands of CBI that we often witness is that teachers may formulate sound language objectives in a CBI lesson, but fail to address them as the procedures and assessment of the lesson unfold. Avoiding the stark division of language and content requires formulating contextualized language objectives and ensuring that they are addressed in the lesson procedures. Sometimes the language objectives are assumed to be met by the mere appearance of language forms in some of the materials, but we do not believe that this is sufficient. For example, if a lesson objective is to focus on conditional sentences, we do not consider the form sufficiently taught if the lesson asks students to read a paragraph where conditionals incidentally appear. Although it is possible that learners may incidentally notice (Schmidt, 2001) the structure of conditionals, our position is that the teacher may need to be more proactive in directing or attracting learners' attention to the new form (Doughty & Williams, 1998). Deliberate planning is essential for balance and integration in CBI.

Review of CBI Models

The shift in paradigm from a structural syllabus to CBI left many open questions about how and when language should be explicitly addressed in instruction. Although CBI may have begun as a rather amorphous approach with vague notions of learning language through content, it has over the years drawn the attention of many researchers who have analyzed more clearly delineated components that are or should be present in CBI instruction.

The concept of language functions has been at the forefront since early theoretical conceptualizations of CBI, as in Mohan's (1986) seminal framework for underlying knowledge structures, an organizing framework for developing language and content thinking skills across the curriculum. Mohan was one of the first to urge the careful analysis of language needed to perform functions across the curriculum and the importance of using visual

MARTHA BIGELOW, SUSAN RANNEY, and ANNE DAHLMAN

representations to facilitate students' understanding of both the language and the content.[1]

In the area of linguistic analysis, functional grammar (Halliday, 1985; Lock, 1996) emphasizes the close link between forms and meanings and the choices that language provides to fulfill any given function, as well as how meaning changes with syntactic and lexical choices. Thinking about language in this way can provide an impetus for teaching language forms in conjunction with meaningful content and with functions in mind. As Lock points out, functional grammar and focus-on-form techniques provide ways to include language instruction in meaningful communicative instruction, thus filling the gaps of structural grammar teaching, which focused narrowly on the forms in isolation, as well as communicative language teaching, which has sometimes rejected any explicit attention to grammatical forms in instruction. A functional grammar approach can be used for analysis of academic texts used in content-based approaches, as in a recent study by Schleppegrell, Achugar, and Oteíza (2004) in which they deconstructed the language of history texts. This approach holds much promise as a tool for analysis of dense academic texts, although the authors warn that it would be overwhelming for teachers to carry out such detailed analysis for the whole text.

Another useful analytic tool for language structures is the well-known pie chart for linguistic forms developed by Larsen-Freeman (2001). This pie chart encourages analysis of grammatical structures in terms of the formal aspects, the meaning of the structure, and the use of the structure in context. These approaches to linguistic analysis demonstrate that decontextualized structural instruction is not faithful to how language structures are used, as well as being ineffective in fostering language acquisition.

Language functions also came to the forefront of planning for instruction with the development of the CALLA approach (Chamot & O'Malley, 1994) and with TESOL's (1997) development of *ESL Standards for Pre-K-12 Students*. CALLA conceptualizes academic language in terms of functions.

> In our view, academic language consists primarily of the language *functions* needed for authentic academic content. Academic language functions are the tasks that language users must be able to perform in the different content areas.… academic language involves using language functions such as identifying and describing content information, explaining a process, analyzing and synthesizing concepts, justifying opinions, or evaluating knowledge. (p. 40)

Similarly, TESOL's formulation of standards relies exclusively on language functions in its identification of specific targets for language instruction through the descriptors (e.g., persuading, arguing, negotiating) used to elaborate the meaning of the broader goals; no language structures are specified. However, the academic language that ELLs need to master is characterized not only by language functions, but also by the use of complex syntax and vocabulary in carrying out these functions.

A functional grammar approach expects teachers to analyze how language functions may be performed with various structures, with the assumption that the choice of structure influences meaning (Halliday, 1985). Gibbons (1991) notes that "within any of the language functions there are many ways of expressing a similar idea" (p. 15) and that the choice of wording affects meaning by changing the focus. She further argues that learners may be limited by being able to express functions in one way only, whereas academic language demands access to complex ways of performing language functions. Her framework for CBI addresses this issue by including separate categories for both language functions and language structures, along with topics, activities, and vocabulary. The framework posits these categories as parallel lists that are connected through slots, as in the sentence: "The topic ____ includes these activities ____ which require these language functions ____ which will be modeled using this language ____" (Gibbons, 1991, p. 19).

Others have also proposed models for analyzing instruction in CBI and ensuring that both language and content are included. Snow et al. (1989) proposed a conceptual framework in which language-learning objectives have three sources: the ESL curriculum, the content area curriculum, and assessment of learners' academic and communicative needs and ongoing evaluation of their language skills. These lead to two types of language objectives: content obligatory and content compatible; the content obligatory objectives focus on the grammar, vocabulary, and functions necessary to learn the content of the lesson, and the content compatible objectives focus on other language items that may be used in the lesson, but are not essential to learning the content.

Short's (2002) model serves to show researchers and practitioners how intertwined and multidimensional the many aspects of CBI as carried out in sheltered content settings can be. Short conceptualizes CBI in three overlapping circles: Task, Content (social studies in this case), and Language. In this framework, content includes both the subject area content and cognitive learning strategies; language includes forms, functions, and language learning strategies; and task refers to content tasks that help students practice or apply content knowledge. This model adeptly captures the complexity of the areas that need to be included in CBI.

Operating from a foreign language perspective, Curtain and Martínez (1990) suggest a planning process where teachers consider "(a) the language skills needed by the students, (b) the content skills that will correlate with the language skills, and (c) the cognitive skills that are necessary to complete the lesson" (p. 204). They recommend beginning with identifying language needed for the particular subject area and then planning hands-on tasks for helping students understand the content concepts. This advice seems particularly appropriate for foreign-language teachers. However, in ESL settings, the planning process must be much more flexible given the frequent need to begin with content materials.

A blueprint for teaching English language development that focuses on ESL classes operating alongside sheltered content was developed by Dutro and Moran (2003). Their model helps practitioners envisage language learning in stand-alone ESL classes or in content instruction where there is front-loading (preteaching) of language prior to the content lesson, as well as advice to take advantage of teachable moments during content instruction to fill specific needs for words or ways to express ideas. In their framework for ESL instruction, they list three main design features: function (related to task), forms (tools for carrying out the task), and fluency (opportunities for practice and application).

From this brief review of some of the more prominent models and frameworks, it is evident that the thinking in the field about CBI has progressed from vague notions of learning language through engagement with age-appropriate academic content to a more clearly determined analysis of what CBI involves and how to plan for it. The issue of balance between content and language in CBI has received a fair amount of attention, and several components have been identified repeatedly in these frameworks: content tasks and activities, language forms and functions, vocabulary, and learning strategies. There seems to be some degree of consensus that these components are important and should be in balance with each other and that planning for CBI entails an analysis of the intersection between linguistic needs and content materials and activities. The frameworks differ in the precise conceptualization of the components of CBI and their interrelationship to each other. The concept of language varies from being represented as predominantly language functions (Chamot & O'Malley, 1994); TESOL *Standards* (1997); or composed of functions, structures, and vocabulary that are either visualized as parallel lists (Dutro & Moran, 2003; Gibbons, 1991) or joined in a single category (Short, 2002; Snow et al., 1989). There are also variations in how the process of planning is conceived—starting from content in some and from language in others.

Our connections model of language and content integration arose from dialogue with ESL teachers and among ourselves and has been used in preliminary collaboration with practicing ESL teachers. The Connections Model is our way of conceptualizing a CBI model that has the flexibility needed to facilitate language teaching in a range of settings and may work to address the challenges CBI has faced in the past, namely, losing the language as content objectives predominate in the instructional process. This model has benefited from the work that has gone before on CBI, but organizes the elements somewhat differently in order to address the need for ESL instruction not only to address both language and content, but to adapt to a variety of contexts. In addition, we strove for simplicity in order to facilitate teachers' planning for the complex challenges of CBI.

The Connections Model: A Model for Planning Content-Based Instruction

We see three principal and interwoven elements in any contextualized language lesson: the content, which encompasses the content texts and the tasks that students are asked to perform as they engage with the content; the language functions that are present in the content texts and that students carry out in the tasks; and the language structures, including grammatical forms and vocabulary that can be found in the content texts and that are used in the process of accomplishing the task and performing the task-based language functions. The relationship between structures and functions can be described as one where a structure represents the linguistic or grammatical form in an utterance and the function denotes the functional intention of that structure, its meaning, and use (Larsen-Freeman, 2001; Sinclair & Coulthard, 1975). Our model posits a dynamic relationship among these three elements, with learning strategies connecting the corners of the triangle, which we call bases.

Under academic language structures, we include grammar, vocabulary, and text organization as distinct but interrelated language structures even though other models of integration (Dutro & Moran, 2003; Gibbons, 1991) separate grammar and vocabulary. Although language *forms* have generally been assumed to focus on formal aspects of morphology and syntax, the workings of particular grammar *structures* depend heavily on lexical features, as in the interplay between the stative/active features of verbs and the use of the progressive aspect (e.g., the ungrammaticality of the progressive aspect with stative verbs such as *to know*). Halliday (1985) makes the point that syntax and vocabulary form a "lexicogrammar", and Celce-Murcia and Larsen-Freeman (1999) argue that grammar and lexicon are linked at opposite ends of a single continuum. For example, one can hardly teach the grammatical features of prepositions, adjectives, or logical connectors without teaching the meanings of the words that fall into those categories. Teaching vocabulary by building word families (i.e., beauty, beautiful, beautifully) involves attention to the grammatical uses of morphology, whereas teaching grammar meaningfully must involve some attention to semantic features of words such as count/non-count nouns. We also include text organization such as discourse patterns of reference and paragraph organization in the category of structures because they are formal patterns of the language, albeit on a broader level than the sentence.

MARTHA BIGELOW, SUSAN RANNEY, and ANNE DAHLMAN

On the other hand, we chose to separate language functions and structures in recognition that both are distinct yet essential aspects of language. Although it is true that the two must inevitably be linked, as it is not possible to perform language functions without language structures, there is a danger in simply assuming that academic language structures will be taught if one plans to teach only language functions. In our experience, when language is conceived as functions only (as in the TESOL *Standards*), specific attention to the forms used for those functions is often overlooked, so it can become difficult for teachers both to ensure that students develop the complex structures that are part of academic English and to integrate grammatical instruction in meaningful content. Alternatively, without considering both language structures and functions, the language structures that teachers often choose do not relate to the content meaningfully because teachers have not considered their connection if any to the main knowledge structures in the text, manifested in language functions, which comprise the main meaning of the text. We also did not want to lump structures and functions together in one category because we saw that teachers would then pick and choose either one in their planning without necessarily making connections between them. Although other models (Dutro & Moran, 2003; Gibbons, 1991) include both language functions and language structures as separate categories, they present them as parallel rather than of interactive categories. In practice, teachers may make the links between these categories when using these models, but we have also seen instruction that targets language functions and structures disjointedly, and we wished to devise a model this addresses that problem through planning processes.

A key feature of our model is what lies between the three main components: double-headed arrows and strategies. The use of arrows signifies that the components need to be closely linked to each other and that teachers should consider each element of the model in relation to the other parts. In effect, it asks teachers to go back and forth between content, language functions, and structures so that they all align well. The strategies are placed along the arrows to indicate that learning strategies provide links between the various components. Learner strategies can and should be explicitly taught, but not simply as a body of knowledge to be mastered. Rather, they provide the means for moving from one type of knowledge to another. Again, it is especially important for teachers to make the connections between learning strategies and the language structures, language functions, and content.

To illustrate the three elements, consider a lesson in an ESL class on the topic of pollution. The teacher could start to plan by thinking about content and moving from there to functions and then structures. A typical *content* task would be for students to write a report about the effect of water pollution on marine animals. The report would require the use of academic language functions such as describing a condition and explaining cause and effect relations. As explained above, any function is carried out through the language structures, and cause and effect could be expressed through a variety of structures such as logical connectors (because, so, as a result) or verbs (cause, resulted in), as in "Water pollution may harm marine animals because it can kill their food source." We include vocabulary, sentence-level syntax, and the larger discourse level (e.g., paragraph, essay organization) in this category. Moving to strategies, students could be guided to use any number of strategies to move through the lesson (for lists of learner strategies, see Chamot & O'Malley, 1994; Chamot, Bernhardt, El-Dinary, & Robbins, 1999; Oxford, 1990; and goal 3 of each of the TESOL *Standards*). For example, they could be taught to use the strategy of selective attention by looking at examples of sentences in a text about pollution with logical connectors and paying particular attention to patterns involving the use of logical connectors to express cause and effect. In this way, students could be taught to use the learning strategy of selective attention to move from structures to functions within the content theme. These components are captured in the model depicted in Figure 1 and serve as an aid to lesson planning that integrates all three aspects.

The model is adaptable to many planning scenarios because any of the three bases could serve as an entry point to the process of planning a lesson.

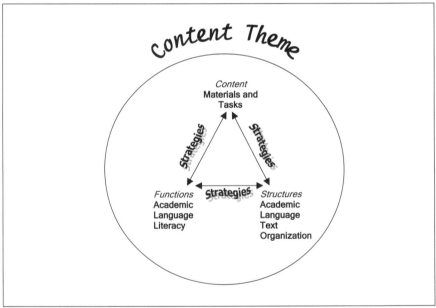

Figure 1. The Connections Model: A flexible planning model for content and language integration in CBI.

MARTHA BIGELOW, SUSAN RANNEY, and ANNE DAHLMAN

For example, in CBI, teachers often begin their planning by designing a language-learning activity or task around the content. In order to ensure that there is attention to academic language development, the teacher could move from this point on the model to consider more deeply the structure and function points of the model. It is possible that teachers could engage the use of academic structures and functions simply by virtue of having chosen a strong language learning task. However, it is also possible that students who lack sophisticated academic language will accomplish the function minimally using their current language abilities, thus losing an opportunity to push their linguistic development through scaffolded instruction that urges them into their zone of proximal development (Vygotsky, 1986).

Teachers who wish to plan some lessons to address some of the language difficulties they have noticed in their students are likely to come into the model via structures. The model can remind teachers to connect structures to content and functions as a way of expanding lessons to ensure a meaningful, content-based context for the language objectives. The model assumes that language needs can be a starting point in a theme-based curriculum, much as in Snow et al.'s (1989) framework. This planning model attempts to help teachers conceptually and practically with the integration of these aspects of language teaching in a more holistic, sustained, and balanced way by keeping the linkages between structures, functions, and content at the forefront of teachers' planning processes. It also aims to encourage a sustained content focus in ESL instruction by always connecting the structures and function with content.

The model also responds to a danger inherent in instruction that relies solely on functions or content. One may assume that if we plan challenging tasks and target appropriate academic language functions, the language will naturally follow; however, as stated above, it is possible for most tasks or functions to be carried out with a minimum of language and certainly without academic language (compare Gibbons, 1991). For example, the function of persuasion could be carried out with a reasoned argument expressed in sophisticated language or it could be expressed in a simple phrase such as "You should believe this." Furthermore, starting from the academic functions targeted in the TESOL *Standards* does not guarantee that the lesson will advance students' academic language skills because language functions such as describing, explaining, and asking questions are also performed in social conversational interaction using basic language structures.

Applications of the Planning Model to a Content-Based Unit

To illustrate the use of the model, we present below a series of lesson ideas based on authentic content derived from an actual adventure learning curriculum that was designed for use in mainstream classes, but that has also been used in ESL classes. We illustrate these lesson ideas by departing from each of the three bases during our modeling of the planning process, that is, content, functions, and structures. This curriculum was developed to follow an expedition team as they crossed the Arctic on dogsleds in 2003-2004. The team posted reports on a Web site that could be accessed by classrooms, and the developers also provided extended materials and Web chats for instruction in topics such as the language and culture of the Inuit people, the Arctic climate, and the natural resources of the area.

Moving from Content to Functions and Structures

For classes that are driven by content (e.g., a sheltered-content class), perhaps the most common starting point in CBI is a content-based text or task. We define *task* broadly as any kind of engagement with the content that encompasses a beginning, middle, and end: a bounded unit of sorts. Tasks can be based on any of the modes or a combination thereof. For example, tasks can focus on comprehension of a text or on completing a group activity. We illustrate this with a sample text and task from a chapter describing the Inuit (*Arctic Transect*, Doenng, 2004, Unit 4).

> *Sample Text*
> *Seasonal Travel.* Traditionally, the Inuit lived in small groups of related families. Communities were located close to important seasonal hunting grounds. Living and surviving meant traveling to find and harvest animals. Families moved inland in the fall to hunt caribou. Later, during freeze up, they fished for arctic char. Seal hunting was done in winter and spring along coastal areas and summer meant finding bird eggs.
> (p. 2)

Academic work typically presents texts such as this for students to read and draw information from. This particular text may present some challenges for English language learners due to the use of language structures that are found more commonly in academic language than in less formal contexts. For example, the text uses the passive voice (*seal hunting was done*), nominalization through gerunds (*living and surviving*), and a complicated pattern of reference with several nouns and pronouns referring to the Inuit. In order for students to draw meaning from this written text, they may need some instruction targeted to these language structures.

A teacher following our planning model could start from the *content text* as a point of departure, consider the *function* of gaining information or more specifically identifying what the paragraph is mainly about, and then choose to focus on the *structure* of reference in this discourse. The teacher would then plan instructional strategies to scaffold students' understanding that the *Inuit, communities, families,* and *they* all refer to the same group of people and that sentences three and six ("Living and surviving meant traveling to find and harvest animals" and "Seal hunting was done in winter and spring along coastal areas and summer meant finding bird eggs") imply the Inuit as unstated agents. The teacher could plan to use the instructional strategy of mapping the pattern of reference through guided reading. To help students understand the structures of passive voice and nominalization in "seal hunting was done in winter and spring," the teacher could instruct students to use *learning strategies* such as activating or cultivating background knowledge to understand that hunting is done by people rather than seals and could instruct students in the strategy of visualizing by making graphic organizers in mapping out the pattern in the sentence. Thus the teacher identifies the content (the analysis of the given text) and then the functions (identifying the main actors in the text) and then the structures (text pattern of reference) using instructional strategies of mapping and guided reading. Students would move from content to functions to structures using learning strategies such as drawing on background knowledge to help them interpret the structure or using visuals such as constructing a map of the pattern.

Starting from a *content task*, we use an example from the *Arctic Transect* (2004) curriculum guide that asks students to read about and create a list of items that people need in order to survive in nature (e.g., positive mental attitude, air, warmth, shelter, rest, etc.). After this, the teacher hands out various hypothetical survival situations on slips of paper and asks students to discuss in their groups what they would do if they were in that situation. The *function* of hypothesizing (a function in Goal 2, Standard 2 in the TESOL *Standards*) is evident, and from there the teacher can plan for instruction on *structures* such as the unreal conditional that could be used to hypothesize. An example of this form is "If I were stranded in the Arctic, I would need shelter." Before letting students begin their discussions, the teacher could draw their attention to the use of the conditional in describing unreal, hypothetical events and provide some initial practice. This step in the planning and instruction process would ensure that students are able to accomplish academic functions and develop competence in academic language. Without this step, there is the possibility that students accomplish the function with a low level of language, but are not pushed toward using more sophisticated academic language. Students could then be encouraged to use the *strategy* of deduction in applying the rules for unreal conditionals in their discussions, as well as the *strategy* of cooperation as they work in groups giving support to each other as they construct hypotheses using appropriate conditional forms.

Moving from Structures to Content and Functions

ESL students often have trouble with word endings, both in terms of grammatical and derivational morphology. We consider this linguistic need to illustrate the path from structure to content and apply it to the above sample text. A teacher could decide that students need instruction on word families and then note that this text contains two examples of adjectives related to nouns (i.e., coastal, seasonal). Using this content text to provide instruction on the linguistic target, the teacher could modify the text by highlighting the targeted words and asking students to use the strategy of inference to make the connections between those adjectives and the related nouns. The vocabulary could be practiced in a content task asking students to describe the Inuit lifestyle using these and other adjectives generated from the activity.

Teachers may choose to start at the entry point of structures for several reasons. They may wish to provide instruction on common problem areas of ELLs of particular first languages (Swan & Smith, 1991) so that they can choose texts and tasks that provide models and practice with these forms. In addition, it is important to consider not only errors, but also the structures that students lack or seem to avoid. For example, students who write short, choppy sentences rather than using the complex sentences that are typical of academic language could benefit from instruction in forming relative clauses or other complex sentences. Another impetus for a focus on particular linguistic forms would be to meet specific language goals that are established by the school district, department, or the teachers themselves. It is important that teachers examine the anticipated linguistic demands of content curriculum in which students are or will be enrolled (Met, 1994). For example, students may need to speculate and infer in social studies class, which creates a good context for learning conditional sentences (e.g., If the northern states had agreed to allow the south to secede, the civil war would have been avoided). Once the grammar structure is targeted, teachers may consider where they could add some instruction in these areas in the context of the content they wish to teach. For example, the grammar objective of "use comparative adjectives correctly" may be integrated with a lesson on measurement or reading graphs in math, and question formation can be integrated into a research activity in social studies.

Moving From Functions to Content and Structures

Functions can provide the point of departure when teachers use the TESOL *Standards* or similar standards as well as when starting from some content texts. We have found that academic language functions are often articulated in many curriculum materials because they are inherent in many objectives and tasks that are presented. For example, some content textbooks list student objectives such as "Students will *compare* and *contrast* two forms of reproduction." Tasks designed for students also often embed functions, as in directions such as "*explain* the scientific method" or "read the paragraph and *predict* what will happen next." In addition, content-area texts are a logical place to see how academic language functions are realized. Thus linking language functions with academic content is generally not problematic.

MARTHA BIGELOW, SUSAN RANNEY, and ANNE DAHLMAN

However, linking content and functions with specific structures takes some additional planning that is often neglected in CBI. All functions are performed through linguistic structures, but in order to promote their expression with advanced academic language, it is helpful to plan to focus the learners on the key structures that they will need to develop proficiency in academic English. To make this link, teachers can observe students carrying out the task effectively and note the language used. For example, in order to perform the function *seek information*, students need to know how to form *wh*-questions. To carry out the function of *compare*, they may need comparative structures and logical connectors such as *on the other hand* or *unlike*. To *order* things, students need to know verb tenses, especially present and past perfect, as well as relevant transition words such as *next, after that*, and so forth. The function of *infer* may be carried out with conditional sentences or with modals such as *may, could*, and *might*. It is important that the teacher ensure, by anticipating during the planning phase, the presentation of a variety of language structures that can be used to carry out a certain language function in order to enable students to practice with higher-level language structures that are typical to academic discourse.

Applying the planning model to our sample curriculum, we consider the example where a teacher has chosen to focus on the function *retelling information*, which is a progress indicator for Goal 2, Standard 2 in the TESOL *Standards*. Using this function as the starting point on the model, the teacher can link it to content and structures in the context of Unit 3 from *Arctic Transect* (2004). The first part of Unit 3 describes the Inuit throat-singing tradition, and the second part is an interview with a famous Inuit throat-singer. The *task* outlined in the curriculum involves a jigsaw reading activity where students work in groups of three or four to read their assigned half, and then present an oral summary of the text to another group that has not read the same information. The group listening to the summary is prompted to ask questions. Thus the task that is offered in the curriculum offers an ideal opportunity for practice with the academic language functions of retelling, summarizing, and asking questions. Going from functions to *structures*, the function of retelling information could lead to the use of indirect speech structures as in "In the Web chat, someone asked if the expedition team had seen a polar bear during their trek." The function of asking for information leads obviously to the structures of yes/no or *wh*-questions. Depending on students' proficiency levels, teachers could also introduce other structures of academic language such as the use of noun clauses in giving information, as in "Living and surviving meant that they had to travel to find and harvest animals." Various *learning strategies* could be applied in moving between the bases of functions and structures as students are challenged to try new structures. For example, students could be encouraged to use the cognitive strategy of practicing naturalistically and the metacognitive strategy of self-monitoring (Oxford, 1990) as they prepare for and carry out their retellings. As we discuss above, these functions could be performed using simpler structures or using the structures inaccurately. If the planning stops at the level of functions, the students might be able to achieve the lesson's objectives without advancing their ability to use academic language. However, if the teacher is conceptualizing the lesson as providing an opportunity to develop academic language structures as well as to practice language functions, he or she can plan to provide some modeling and scaffolding of advanced structures.

What would this approach look like in terms of a syllabus?
Language curricula have passed through many trends, each with a single focus (i.e., the grammatical syllabus, the notional-functional syllabus, the task-based syllabus). CBI calls for a balanced approach between language and content (Nunan, 2001; Stoller, 2002). The starting point in CBI is often content, yet content is a vehicle for language instruction rather than the end in itself, and CBI is sometimes practiced without explicit language instruction. However, we argue that a setting where students are expected to learn language and content needs to make space for deliberate attention to language structures and functions: spaces where it is possible to "teach English, not just teach *in* English" (Dutro & Moran, 2003, p. 228). Often this would involve simply thinking more deliberately about the tasks and texts used in teaching the content or making sure that language objectives are assessed. But it also involves sometimes starting from the language needs of the students and fitting the content to them, as in noticing the errors or omissions in students' output and planning a lesson to address them, or noticing that students have difficulty processing written texts with complex structures.

CBI differs from the grammatical syllabus in that the grammar points would be selected and ordered based on both language and functions that emerge from the content and the students' language learning needs, so they may not seem to follow a linear order from simple to more complex forms. Rather than an ordered list of grammatical items to be taught linearly, grammatical structures in CBI would be taught in a cyclical pattern, with forms being introduced, revisited, and practiced on an ongoing basis as they fit in with the content and functions that are taught. In order to ensure that important structures receive adequate attention, teachers could keep lists of structures that have been taught or check off structures taught from another set of curricular guidelines. More challenging to keep track of are structures that the students are not yet producing. Students can also participate by keeping their own grammar/vocabulary logs and portfolios that track their language development and point to areas that need attention. Specific pedagogical tools for grammar instruction should be varied and include a range of corrective feedback techniques as well as task and text modifications (e.g.,

MARTHA BIGELOW, SUSAN RANNEY, and ANNE DAHLMAN

input enhancement, input flood, input processing tasks, Doughty & Williams, 1998).

This more fluid approach to grammar allows naturally for integration with content. Once teachers see that grammar can be included without having to dominate or direct the flow of content instruction, it will become easier to overcome the problem of grammar being omitted from CBI or taught on a parallel but disconnected track. In addition, strategy instruction should be integrated into the content and language components so that it is seen as a means to learn and connect the various components, rather than an additional set of procedures to be mastered.

Collaborative Curriculum Development

The Connections Model is designed to be used by ESL teachers planning alone or in collaboration with content teachers. Although this type of collaboration can be beneficial, there is a risk that the content curriculum will dominate and leave little space for language development goals and assessment. As noted above, the common tendency of teachers to simplify content lessons so that they are comprehensible does not guarantee language development. In a collaborative team, the ESL teacher needs to focus on ensuring that attention is paid to the development of academic language proficiency. All too often ESL teachers are called on to simplify tasks and texts for ELLs rather than to work with ELLs on the skills they need to cope with challenging tasks and texts while producing more and more complex grammatical structures. Although simplifying language may be a worthy goal, ELLs also need to develop language skills and learning strategies that they can use eventually to access unmodified material (Kinsella, 2002). Oversimplification can hinder learning because students are not exposed to advanced grammatical structures and do not receive instruction in them either.

Some curriculum development teams may find it helpful to start from the functions targeted in the unit. Functions can serve as common ground between content and language specialists because they describe what students are expected to do with the content and with language on a general level. Other starting points can be the givens in the content course. Givens may be the textbook that the teacher is going to use or assignments and projects that are main parts of the culture and tradition of the course. With this information, language specialists can discern what lexical, syntactic, and discourse skills are needed to carry out the task and scaffold English language development accordingly. In this way, the expertise of all involved is used. No matter how the specifics of collaboration work, the Connections Model can help ensure that language instruction is given its due place in CBI and is contextualized in content.

Conclusion

The Connections Model is distinguished by the proposal that in order to achieve a balance between content and language in the curriculum, it is necessary to unpack the language objectives into structures and functions, and carefully tie these objectives to content. Teachers may find that the model asks them to think more about language than they expected. This is intentional. Given the tendency for content to overshadow language objectives in most types of CBI programs, we ask teachers to lean slightly toward the side of language during the planning processes in order to guarantee that language is not lost as the instruction unfolds. At the same time, the model serves to remind teachers to focus on all three aspects of CBI and the connections between them. Again, the emphasis of the model is on trying to restore balance and integration rather than allowing instruction to focus narrowly on one aspect. The model makes the consideration of language more thorough and pushes instruction so that students will expand their repertoires of forms. By investing in this type of planning, where content and language are taught together and where conceptualization of language objectives does not stop with language functions in isolation from structures, teachers can ensure that learners will be better able to make form-meaning connections as they learn academic content in their new language.

Engaging ELLs in activities that promote form-meaning connections through academic content requires teachers to develop a range of pedagogical skills. Specifically, it requires well-developed language awareness including the ability to analyze language structures that are present in authentic texts and the language ELLs produce. It requires the ability to see connections between content and language and between various aspects of language such as structures and functions. Because CBI is an approach that most teachers still have not experienced in their own language learning histories, and because it is not easy to analyze and synthesize curriculum in this multifaceted way, teachers will need many opportunities for guidance and practice with this approach. We offer this planning model as a tool to draw on in the process of practicing CBI such that it fulfills its potential for developing language proficiency that meets the needs of ELLs who are under tremendous pressure to learn academic language and content quickly and successfully. One of most important specialties ESL teachers bring to their work is their knowledge about language. They need to use this professional knowledge in new ways to meet the challenges of teaching in changing contexts and to ensure that their students are supported in their language development.

Note

[1] According to Mohan (1986), activities are core to the knowledge framework in that they serve to provide opportunities for learners to develop skills through an expository approach that is

verbal and explicit. Mohan's notion of the central role of task in language teaching and learning was taken up with great vigor in the field in the late 1980s and early 1990s (Crookes & Gass, 1993; Candlin & Murphy, 1987; Nunan, 1989).

Acknowledgment

The authors acknowledge Diane Tedick, Jennifer Leazer, Karla Stone, and Beth Gregor for extremely helpful feedback and conversation about the model presented in this article.

The Authors

Martha Bigelow is an assistant professor at the University of Minnesota. She has taught English as a second/foreign language in the US, the Dominican Republic, and the Republic of Panama. Her research interests include processes of language teacher learning and instruction for secondary English-language learners with limited formal schooling.

Susan Ranney teaches at the University of Minnesota in the Second Languages and Cultures Education program. She has taught ESL in the US and Nigeria. Her research interests include sociolinguistics and grammar pedagogy.

Anne Dahlman is an assistant professor in educational studies at Minnesota State University, Mankato. Her main research interests are teacher collaboration, academic language proficiency, and standards-based instruction.

References

Candlin, C., & Murphy, D. (Eds.). (1987). *Language learning tasks*. Englewood Cliffs, NJ: Prentice-Hall International.

Celce-Murcia, M., & Larsen-Freeman, D. (1999). *The grammar book: An ESL/EFL teacher's course* (2nd ed.). Boston, MA: Heinle & Heinle.

Chamot, A.U., & O'Malley, J.M. (1994). *The CALLA handbook: Implementing the cognitive academic language learning approach*. New York: Addison-Wesley.

Chamot, A., Bernhardt, S., El-Dinary, P., Robbins, J. (1999). *The learning strategies handbook*. White Plains, NY: Addison-Wesley Longman.

Collier, V. (1989). How long? A synthesis of research on academic achievement in a second language. *TESOL Quarterly, 23*, 509-531.

Crookes, G., & Gass, S. (Eds.). (1993). *Tasks and language learning: Integrating theory and practice*. Clevedon, UK: Multilingual Matters.

Curtain, H.A., & Martínez, L.S. (1990). Content-based instruction in second and foreign languages. In A. Padilla, H.H. Fairchild, & C. Valadez (Eds.), *Foreign language education: Issues and strategies* (pp. 201-221). Newbury Park, CA: Sage.

Doenng, A. (2004). *Adventure learning—Arctic Transect 2004: An educational exploration of Nunavut curriculum*. Available: http://www.polarhusky.com

Doughty, C., & Williams, J. (1998). Pedagogical choices in focus on form. In C. Doughty & J. Williams (Eds.), *Focus on form in classroom SLA* (pp. 197-261). Cambridge, UK: Cambridge University Press.

Dutro, S., & Moran, C. (2003). Rethinking English language instruction: An architectural approach. In G.G. García (Ed.), *English learners: Reaching the highest level of English literacy* (pp. 227-258). Newark, DE: International Reading Association.

Echevarria, J., Vogt, M., & Short, D.J. (2004). *Making content comprehensible for English language learners: The SIOP model*. Boston, MA: Allyn and Bacon.

Genesee, F. (1987). *Learning through two languages: Studies of immersion and bilingual education*. Cambridge, MA: Newbury House.

Gibbons, P. (1991). *Learning to learn in a second language*. Portsmouth, NH: Heinemann.

Gibbons, P. (2002). *Scaffolding language, scaffolding learning*. Portsmouth, NH: Heinemann.

Halliday, M.A.K. (1985). *An introduction to functional grammar*. London: Edward Arnold.

Kinsella, K. (2002). *Reading in the content areas: Strategies for reading success.* Upper Saddle River, NJ: Globe Fearon.

Larsen-Freeman, D. (2001). Teaching grammar. In M. Celce-Murcia (Ed.), *Teaching English as a second or foreign language* (3rd ed., pp. 251-266). Boston, MA: Heinle & Heinle.

Lock, G. (1996). *Functional English grammar: An introduction for second language teachers.* Cambridge, UK: Cambridge University Press.

Master, P. (2000). Grammar in content-based instruction. In L. Kasper (Ed.), *Content-based college ESL instruction* (pp. 93-106). Mahwah, NJ: Erlbaum.

Met, M. (1991). Learning language through content: Learning content through language. *Foreign Language Annals, 24,* 281-295.

Met, M. (1994). Teaching content through a second language. In F. Genesee (Ed.), *Educating second language children: The whole child, the whole curriculum, the whole community* (pp. 159-182). Cambridge, UK: Cambridge University Press.

Mohan, B. (1986). *Language and content.* Reading, MA: Addison-Wesley.

Nunan, D. (1989). *Designing tasks for the communicative classroom.* Cambridge, UK: Cambridge University Press.

Nunan, D. (2001). Syllabus design. In M. Celce-Murcia (Ed.), *Teaching English as a second or foreign language* (3rd ed., pp. 55-65). New York: Heinle & Heinle Thomson Learning.

Oxford, R. (1990). *Language learning strategies: What every teacher should know.* Boston, MA: Heinle & Heinle.

Pica, T. (1995). Teaching language and teaching language teachers. In J.E.A. et al. (Ed.), *Georgetown University round table on language and linguistics 1995* (pp. 378-397). Washington, DC: Georgetown University Press.

Schleppegrell, M.J., Achugar, M., & Oteíza, T. (2004). The grammar of history: Enhancing content-based instruction through a functional focus on language. *TESOL Quarterly, 38,* 67-93.

Schmidt, R.W. (2001). Attention. In P. Robinson (Ed.), *Cognition and second language instruction* (pp. 3-32). Cambridge, UK: Cambridge University Press.

Short, D.J. (2002). Language learning in sheltered social studies classes. *TESOL Journal, 11*(1), 18-24.

Sinclair, J., & Coulthard, M. (1975). *Toward an analysis of discourse.* Oxford, UK: Oxford University Press.

Snow, M.A. (2001). Content-based and immersion models for second and foreign language teaching. In M. Celce-Murcia (Ed.), *Teaching English as a second or foreign language* (3rd ed., pp. 303-318). Boston, MA: Heinle & Heinle.

Snow, M. S., Met, M., & Genesee, F. (1989). A conceptual framework for the integration of language and content in second/foreign language instruction. *TESOL Quarterly, 23,* 201-217.

Stoller, F.L. (2002). Promoting the acquisition of knowledge in a content-based course. In J.A. Crandall & D. Kaufman (Eds.), *Content-based instruction in higher education settings* (pp. 109-123). Alexandria, VA: TESOL.

Stoller, F.L., & Grabe, W. (1997). A six-T's approach to content-based instruction. In M.A. Snow & D.M. Brinton (Eds.), *The content-based classroom: Perspectives on integrating language and content* (pp. 78-94). White Plains, NY: Addison Wesley Longman.

Swan, M., & Smith, B. (Eds.). (1991). *Learner English: A teacher's guide to interference and other problems* (2nd ed.). Cambridge, UK: Cambridge University Press.

TESOL. (1997). *ESL standards for pre-K-12 students.* Alexandria, VA: Author.

VanPatten, B. (1990). Attending to form and content in the input: An experiment in consciousness. *Studies in Second Language Acquisition, 12,* 287-301.

Vygotsky, L. (1986). *Thought and language.* Cambridge, MA: MIT Press.

Individual and Social-Contextual Factors Affecting the Learning and Use of ESL: A Case Study of a Visiting Korean Physician

Su-Ja Kang

This case study examined factors that affected a Korean physician's learning and use of ESL in an English-speaking country, using data from interviews, observations, notebook memos and e-mails. The findings indicated that individual factors-personality (perfectionism and extroversion), occupation, beliefs, and motivation—and social-contextual factors—lack of contact with native speakers and insecurity about speaking English in the presence of other Koreans—influenced the participant's learning and use of ESL. The findings also revealed that the participant's motivation and extroversion played a role in overcoming the social-contextual obstacles limiting learning opportunities, which illustrates interactions between individual and social-contextual factors.

S'appuyant sur des données provenant d'entrevues, d'observations, de notes de service et de courriels, l'auteure étudie les facteurs qui ont influencé l'apprentissage, par un médecin coréen, de l'anglais langue seconde, et l'emploi qu'il faisait de cette langue dans un pays d'expression anglaise. Les résultats indiquent que des critères individuels (caractère perfectionniste ou extraverti; profession; croyances; et motivation) et des facteurs socio-contextuels (manque de contact avec des locuteurs natifs et sentiment d'insécurité devant le fait de parler anglais en présence de Coréens) ont influencé l'apprentissage de l'anglais par le participant et l'emploi qu'il faisait de cette langue. De plus, ils dénotent que la motivation et le caractère extraverti du participant l'ont aidé à surmonter les obstacles socio-contextuels qui limitaient les occasions d'apprentissage, ce qui illustre l'interaction entre les facteurs individuels et socio-contextuels.

Introduction

Second-language acquisition (SLA) researchers have tried to identify the factors influencing language-learning that may lead to either success or failure in language-learning. Some SLA researchers have investigated the relationship between language-learning and individual learner characteristics. According to Skehan (1989), who comprehensively examined individual differences in second-language learning, learning can vary depending on an individual's characteristics such as aptitude, motivation, learning strategies, extroversion-introversion, risk-taking, intelligence, field independence, and anxiety. Oxford (1992) synthesized research on individual differences in language-learning, addressing a wide range of factors that research has indicated to be important: age, sex, motivation, anxiety, self-esteem, tolerance of ambiguity, risk-taking, cooperation, competition, and language-learning strategies and styles, and also provided pedagogical implications (for an additional overview, see Ehrman, Leaver, & Oxford, 2003; Oxford & Ehrman, 1993; Skehan, 1991). Many SLA researchers have examined the relationship between learning strategies and other individual characteristics, especially with regard to the rate of acquisition and the ultimate level of achievement (Ellis, 1994; Green & Oxford, 1995; Oxford, 1989; Oxford & Nyikos, 1989; LoCastro, 2001; Yang, 1999).

Studies investigating individual variables have tried to show, mainly through correlation studies, whether learner characteristics are related to language-learning and if so, how. Findings from correlation studies have been controversial in terms of the existence, direction, and scope of the relationship between these individual factors and learning. For example, a conflict can be found regarding the existence of the link between aptitude and acquisition. Whereas Krashen (1981) stated that aptitude relates only to learning, not to acquisition, Skehan (1989) argued that aptitude plays a role both in formal and informal acquisition environments. A possible explanation for the conflicting finding can be found in Oxford's (1992) statement that certain individual factors (e.g., tolerance of ambiguity and risk-taking) do not always create consistent results for all language learners because the factors interact with other factors (e.g., anxiety, self-esteem, motivation, and learning styles) in a complex way to produce certain effects in language-learning.

Other researchers have investigated the role of contextual factors in language-learning. Politzer's (1983) study, which documented the relationships between learning behavior and achievement, revealed that these may depend heavily on contextual factors such as the type of evaluation (linguistic or communicative tests), course level, and teaching methods. Harklau (1994) found that the interaction routines of spoken and written language use, along with the structure and goal of instruction, were different in two learning environments: ESL versus mainstream classes. Lafford (2004) indicated that learning context—at-home classroom versus study abroad—had a significant effect on the categories of communication strategies and language use of learners of Spanish as a second language. A study by Freed, Segalowitz, and Dewey (2004), which compared regular classroom, study abroad, and intensive domestic immersion programs, also showed that the learning context affected various dimensions of second-language fluency in French. Jacob, Rottenberg, Patrick, and Wheeler (1996) suggested that local contextual features (e.g., students' definition of the task, features of the task, and participant structures) influenced L2 learners' opportunities to acquire academic English in cooperative learning. Sharkey and Layzer (2000) showed how teachers' attitudes, beliefs, and practices facilitate or hinder English learners' access to academic success and resources. Most of these studies investigating the influence of contextual factors compared predetermined factors, mainly regarding academic settings such as learning context, teachers' beliefs and practice, task, evaluation, and teaching materials and methods.

Unlike SLA researchers focusing on only one type of factors, either individual factors or contextual factors, others have proposed that language-learning is related to both types of factors. In Abraham and Vann's (1987) model of second-language-learning, background factors (e.g., age, intelligence, personality, education, and cognitive style) affect the philosophy, approach, and strategies learners use in learning and communication, which directly influence the degree of success or failure. In this model, environmental factors surrounding the second-language-learning experience (e.g., formal/informal instruction and practice) were suggested affective factors having an indirect effect on the degree of learning success. In a similar vein, Ellis's (1994) model of L2 acquisition proposed that learners' choice of learning strategies is determined by individual differences (e.g., beliefs, affective states, learner factors, and learning experiences) and various situational factors (e.g., target language, (in)formal setting, instruction, and task), and social factors (e.g., socioeconomic status and sex). MacIntyre (1994) also argued that "a model of strategy use should include individual and situational variables" (p. 188). The influence of both individual and contextual factors was revealed in El-Dib's (2004) study, which found a relationship between sex and language level and proposed that learning context in a cultural milieu is perhaps the strongest variable affecting the choice of strategy.

Drawing on the views suggested by Abraham and Vann (1987), Ellis (1994), and MacIntyre (1994), my assumption throughout the current study has been that an individual's language-learning and use can be influenced by both individual and contextual factors, especially social-contextual factors. The individual factors in this study are similar to the background factors in Abraham and Vann's model in that both refer to characteristics pertaining to an individual. Because the participant Sungwoo's strongest desire was to learn spoken English through social interactions with native speakers, this study focused on social-contextual factors. However, unlike the environmental and situational factors in these other models, which appeared to focus on the variations in educational setting and instruction, I use the term *social-contextual factors* to refer to environmental factors pertaining to the social context of learning. In accordance with MacIntyre's (1994) statement that "the use of strategies ... seems to depend on the interaction of learner characteristics and the demands of the situation" (p. 187), I have also assumed that there may be an interaction between individual and social-contextual factors.

Although SLA researchers have suggested the possible influence of both individual and environmental (Abraham & Vann, 1987) or situational factors (Ellis, 1994), and the interaction among them (MacIntyre, 1994), no studies have actually examined the two types of factors together, including the interaction between these two types. Because the prior research was mainly conducted using quantitative methods, we also lack qualitative descriptive data.

Finally, many studies have focused on ESL (English as a second language) students and adult immigrants. To date, however, no studies have examined Korean physicians who stay in an English-speaking country as visiting scholars. As pointed out by LoCastro (1994), it is doubtful whether the list of learning strategies based on immigrants and ESL students can apply to L2 learners with different educational and social backgrounds. Findings from many studies examining ESL students and adult immigrants may not apply to a visiting Korean physician. This is because the language-learning of physicians who come to an English-speaking country to conduct research and are later expected to return to their jobs in their home countries would be different from that of immigrants who are planning to make their homes in English-speaking countries, or from that of ESL students who come to English-speaking countries to take ESL classes in intensive language programs. The above-mentioned gaps in the literature have provided the rationale for conducting this study.

This study explored individual and social-contextual factors that influenced a visiting Korean physician's learning and use of ESL in an English-speaking country, addressing the following research questions.
1. In what ways, if any, do individual factors affect the learning and use of ESL?
2. In what ways, if any, do social-contextual factors affect the learning and use of ESL?
3. In what ways, if any, do individual and social-contextual factors interact with each other?

Method

The Participant

The participant, Sungwoo, is a Korean gynecologist in his 40s and a professor in a medical school in Korea. He came to an English-speaking country, the United States, with his wife and two daughters as a visiting scholar. Although Sungwoo came here to conduct research, the most important goal he wished to achieve during his stay was to improve his spoken English skills by communicating with native speakers. Because of the strong desire to achieve his goal, he was highly motivated to learn English, especially spoken English. To improve his spoken English, he made an effort to learn English outside his workplace by attending ESL classes provided in the community and meeting with a literacy volunteer.

For the first six months of his stay, Sungwoo conducted research in a laboratory where all his colleagues were non-native speakers, including the director. As a result of his effort to find a new workplace where he could work with native speakers, he began working in a hospital from the seventh month of his stay. In the hospital, he mainly observed consulting rooms and operating rooms without practicing. He also conducted some research in the hospital laboratory. While he was working in the hospital, he had more opportunities to communicate in English with native speakers than in his previous workplace.

In Korea, Sungwoo took English classes in school starting in grade 7, the first year of middle school. Under the old traditional English education system before the recent introduction of the innovative communicative approach, he mainly learned written English in school, focusing on grammar and reading skills. He always received good grades on written English tests at school, which gave him confidence in written English. Sungwoo's English learning experience at school in Korea, however, was missing one important part of English proficiency, spoken English skills. Through the experience of meeting English-speaking patients and attending international conferences, he realized the importance of spoken English. Before coming to an English-speaking country, he had made efforts to improve his spoken English skills by attending private language institutes in order to learn spoken English from native speakers, getting some private tutoring from native speakers, and watching videotapes made for English-language-learning.

The Role of the Researcher

As Butterworth and Hatch (1978) did in their study, I tried to build a close friendship with Sungwoo and his family. I invited them to my home or to restaurants to build rapport. My family also had several chances to make one-day trips and spend the entire day with his family. In so doing, I could observe him in a variety of situations and was able to conduct informal interviews about his everyday experiences. My family also helped him whenever he needed help. We corrected his e-mails written in English and helped with phone calls to native speakers of English. In several cases, we had to accompany him as interpreters, especially when he was involved in some important matters such as working on contracts. Through this close relationship between his family and mine, I was able to collect data in a wide variety of contexts.

Data Collection and Analysis

Data collection began when Sungwoo had been in the US for about four months and continued through 13 months of his stay. Although data were collected only during this period, this study investigated Sungwoo's experiences regarding the first four months of his 17-month stay. Data about his experiences during his first four months were collected during interviews in which Sungwoo often mentioned his first four months' experiences. He kept dated records in his memo notebook, which was another source of data for his experiences during the first four months of his sojourn.

For triangulation, various types of data were gathered and used in the research analysis. I conducted formal interviews; I also collected data in informal interviews during daily interactions with him on a personal level. Some of the data were collected during phone calls when he also reflected on his experiences. I made observations in various contexts such as ESL classes, a literacy volunteer's place, and on other social occasions during which he used English. Another source of data was his memo notebook in which he wrote English vocabulary and expressions.

All the formal and informal interviews were conducted in Korean to avoid losing data because of the participant's inability to express himself in English. All the formal interviews were audiotaped. I tried to write down informal interviews that were not audiotaped as soon as possible after they occurred. Interviews were first transcribed in Korean and then translated into English. The informal interview data transcribed in Korean were taken to the participant for member checks. During this process, he made corrections and added more information to the transcript.

Data analysis was an ongoing process conducted throughout the study, as recommended by Merriam (1998). Data were initially coded to identify emerging themes about the participant's language use, learning experiences, and affective factors. I first identified recurrent characteristics of his language use and learning. After that, I identified individual and social-contextual factors that were emerging in relation to those recurrent characteristics, establishing connections between them on the basis of a logical chain of evidence (Miles & Huberman, 1994).

To develop the trustworthiness of the study, some of Merriam's (1998) basic strategies were used. For purposes of triangulation, the data were collected from multiple sources. A member check was also conducted by taking tentative findings and interpretations to the participant and asking him if they were plausible. As a means of peer evaluation, I frequently asked colleagues to comment on the findings as they emerged. In order to identify the researcher's biases, the researcher's assumptions were clarified at the outset of the study.

Findings

Sungwoo's learning and use of ESL were influenced both by individual factors such as his perfectionist and extroverted personality, occupation, learning beliefs, and motivation, and by two social-contextual factors: lack of contact with native speakers and insecurity about speaking English in the presence of Koreans. Moreover, there were interactions between his individual factors—motivation and extroversion—and the social-contextual factors. Due to these interactions, through the role of extroversion and motivation, he was able to overcome to some degree the social-contextual obstacles limiting his opportunities to speak and learn English.

Individual Factors

Influence of perfectionism on the desire to speak correct English

Sungwoo's perfectionist personality affected his language use, more specifically his desire to speak correct English. Sungwoo's perfectionist personality was revealed in his statement, "I think I try to be perfect in everything I do." The following excerpt shows his desire to speak correct English, which also contributed to his fear of speaking incorrectly.

> I only want to say perfect sentences. I believe that we should say correct sentences like those in textbooks. I know it hinders my English learning. Due to my desire to speak in correct expressions, I speak less often than do others. I often miss opportunities to speak, figuring out the correct word order of the sentence.... When I come up with the correct words to say, it is too late to say them because they are already talking about something else.

Sungwoo's desire to speak correct sentences can be understood in relation to Jorden's (1977) statement that error avoidance might to some extent be psychologically determined; some language users feel bad about communicating in a foreign language unless they can do so without exhibiting linguistic handicaps. As expressed in this excerpt, Sungwoo's desire to speak correct English contributed to his reluctance to take risks, which in turn limited his opportunities to speak English. Drawing on the fact that Sungwoo is an extrovert, which is discussed below, this finding is unexpected and cannot be explained by the findings of earlier studies that extroverts are less likely to be reluctant to take risks. This mismatch illustrates that predicting language learners' behaviors and learning outcomes based on one characteristic (extroversion in this study), without consideration of other related characteristic(s) (perfectionism in this study) can be inaccurate.

Sungwoo's desire to speak correct English was also rooted in his belief that English should be spoken correctly. This belief was reflected when he talked about another visiting scholar in the hospital from Greece.

> My friend from Greece, he speaks a lot although his English is terrible. I often don't understand what he is saying and native speakers of English don't seem to understand him either. Nonetheless, he keeps talking. I feel bad for him. He doesn't seem to care about how he looks or realize

how often he looks bad. But I am different from him. I learned good English and it annoys me to speak incorrect English.

Sungwoo's desire to speak correct English appeared to come from his perfectionism, as expressed in the following excerpt.

Usually, I tried to be faultless. For example, I tend to wait 30 minutes even after I confirmed somebody died. Even though I am pretty sure he or she died, I tell the family after 30 minutes.... I want to be perfect in speaking English too. I feel bad about speaking incorrect English sentences.... When speaking English, I feel like a different person, I mean, no longer a perfect person as I am in other matters.

As Sungwoo wished to be faultless or perfect in everything, he also developed a desire to speak perfect English. The fact that he wished to have his e-mail messages written in English proofread also reflects his desire to use correct English.

The finding that Sungwoo's perfectionist characteristic affected his desire to speak correct English is consistent with Brophy's (1996) argument that "perfectionists … are more concerned about avoiding mistakes than about learning" (p. 112), and Gregersen and Horwitz's (2002) observation that "perfectionist students … would want to speak flawlessly, with no grammatical or pronunciation errors" (p. 563).

Influence of Occupation on the Fear of Speaking Incorrectly

As Sungwoo's perfectionism influenced his desire to speak correct English, his occupation as a physician played a role in his fear of speaking incorrectly. Sungwoo related how and why mistakes are not allowed in medical science.

We medical doctors deal with human lives. A small mistake can cause serious damage to a human's life. That's why we medical doctors must be faultless. Any fault is not allowed in my field. As I have lived this way, I am not accustomed to doing or saying something incorrect. So I am afraid to speak incorrect English sentences. It's very uncomfortable when I realize that I produce incorrect English sentences when I am speaking English.

This excerpt shows that Sungwoo's fear of speaking English incorrectly was related to his occupation. It needs to be emphasized, however, that his field of study did not seem to be the only reason why he developed this fear. Some physicians do not seem to fear speaking incorrect English. According to Sungwoo, for example, although the visiting scholar from Greece spoke careless English, he did not seem to be bothered by it. Based on this, I argue that Sungwoo's fear of speaking incorrectly was shaped not only by the role of his profession as a physician, but also by his desire to speak correct English, which was attributable to his perfectionist personality.

Influence of Occupation on the Desire to Speak Formally and Politely

Sungwoo's occupation also deeply influenced his language use and desire to learn and speak formal and polite English. Sungwoo strongly believed that as a doctor, he should learn formal and polite English, as illustrated in the following excerpt:

> I want to learn formal and polite English. I mean, I want to learn decent English that is not rude. So I told the literacy volunteer that I want to learn decent English. I don't want to speak English casually and carelessly. Because I want to learn good English, I told the literacy volunteer that I wanted to learn good English rather than just communicating with words…. she has tried to teach me formal expressions. For example, she told me that I should say "May I use it?" rather than "Can I use it?" I very often ask her whether or not some expression can be considered rude and what is a polite expression that can be used instead of the rude expression if it is a rude expression.

Sungwoo explained why he needed to use formal expressions as a doctor:

> I am a doctor, specifically a gynecologist. All my patients are women. Unlike American women, many Korean women are very shy. Many patients come to me with agony. They come to me because they are sick. Very often, they also have to say something that is difficult for them to talk about. I think I should be very gentle to them…. I believe that one of a doctor's jobs is to make patients feel respected so that they are comfortable speaking about their problems and concerns. In order to do that, I should not speak informally and impolitely. In addition, I need to explain to them about their symptoms, which should be delivered clearly without any misunderstanding. In order to do that, I think when I see an English speaking patient in Korea, I should use easy, appropriate, and polite expressions in English as well as in Korean.

The excerpt shows that Sungwoo's desire to learn formal and polite English was rooted in his profession, in which doctors are expected to use formal and polite expressions while conversing with their patients.

Influence of Beliefs About Language-Learning on the Use of Language-Learning Strategies

Sungwoo's beliefs about language-learning, developed in Korea, influenced his use of language-learning strategies in an English-speaking country. At the outset, Sungwoo developed these beliefs through his initial training in study habits from his father and from his English teachers during his school years. In a personal conversation, Sungwoo described his father.

I learned from my father that every field of study should be studied by memorization.... When reading newspapers, he always looked up words in the Chinese dictionary. I still remember it clearly.... He was interested in English, too. He always asked my brothers and me about pronunciation and meaning of words.... If something came up in his mind or he came across some expressions, he wrote it down in his notebook. If he couldn't understand something in the newspaper, he looked it up in the dictionary. If he couldn't understand economics, for example, he looked it up in the dictionary and he called his friend's house whose son was majoring in economics to find out the meaning of the term. That's my father. All of these are still vivid to me.... My father influenced my beliefs about effective ways of studying English.

This excerpt shows that Sungwoo's father strongly influenced his learning beliefs about note-taking, looking up words in the dictionary, memorization, confirmation, and asking for help. When I asked Sungwoo whether his English teachers at school encouraged him to use the same strategies as his father did, Sungwoo answered that his English teachers encouraged similarly. Although he admitted that he was influenced both by his father and his teachers, he seemed to believe that his father's influence was the stronger. His successful experiences of receiving high scores on written English tests using these strategies must have contributed to solidifying his beliefs about the usefulness of these strategies.

Sungwoo's field of study also reinforced his beliefs about language-learning. When asked why he believed memorization was the best way to learn English, he replied,

I have memorized for the last 40 years. In my field, we need to memorize everything. In order to memorize later, everything should be written down. Through this experience, probably, that's why I believe memorization is the best way to learn English.

It appears that Sungwoo solidified learning beliefs developed during his school years while studying medical science in college. Because studying in his field required the same strategies he used for language-learning, such as note-taking and memorization, Sungwoo's beliefs about language-learning seemed to be reinforced. This finding that Sungwoo's field of study contributed to his beliefs about language-learning, which in turn affected his use of language-learning strategies, lends support to the influence of university major on the selection of language-learning strategies (Oxford & Nyikos, 1989).

While learning spoken English in an English-speaking country, he activated his language-learning beliefs and used strategies that he had believed to be the best ways to study written English, although how much he relied on these strategies fluctuated over time. Sungwoo used a note-taking strategy, as stated in the following comment.

I write down some expressions that are used between doctors and patients while I am observing them. Today I wrote down "sit up." … I tried to write down the expressions immediately after I got out of the examining room. Sometimes, I could make it, but sometimes I didn't because I forgot and other times I had to do something right after that.

Figure 1 shows parts from Sungwoo's memo notebook that vividly show his note-taking strategies.

As shown in example (1), Sungwoo wrote down expressions that he heard other doctors using when they examined a patient. He also copied some sentences from the newspapers as in example (2). As shown in examples (3) and (4), when he ran across unknown words, he wrote down the words with their phonetic descriptions and meanings, which he looked up in the dictionary. In example (3), he wrote down the phonetic descriptions and meanings of unknown words on the menu in a restaurant. In example (4), he copied a sentence from a news caption on television and wrote down the phonetic descriptions and meanings of the unknown words. These examples show not only his note-taking strategies, but also dictionary consulting strategies.

Sungwoo also related why he used the note-taking strategy.

I wrote down some expressions in order to memorize and use them in later conversations … I write down expressions that I hear or see somewhere, but I do not know their meanings in order to check in the dictionary or ask about them later.

In this excerpt, his memorization and confirmation learning strategies were expressed. His confirmation strategy was also revealed when he explained why he chose to meet the literacy volunteer instead of going to ESL classes on the day the two schedules overlapped. Sungwoo said, "I go to see the volunteer because I can ask specific questions, for example, whether some expressions are correct and formal expressions, which I cannot ask easily in ESL classes." His use of confirmation strategy was frequently observed in his meeting with the literacy volunteer.

This finding about the relationship between Sungwoo's beliefs and language-learning strategies is consistent with Yang (1999). Yang found that language learners' self-efficacy beliefs about learning English were strongly related to their use of all types of learning strategies, especially functional practice strategies, and that their beliefs about the value and nature of learning spoken English were closely linked to their use of formal oral-practice strategies.

Social-Contextual Factors

Influence of lack of contact with native speakers on limiting learning opportunities
Sungwoo's language-learning was influenced by one social-contextual factor, lack of contact with native speakers, which limited his opportunities to speak and learn English through interactions with them. With a strong desire to improve his spoken English skills, Sungwoo wished to interact with native speakers as much as possible. Unfortunately, he did not have much contact with native speakers, especially during the first six months when he worked in the laboratory where there were no native speakers. Although Sungwoo tried to find opportunities to speak English with native speakers outside his workplace, it was hard for him to have contact with native speakers other than salespersons in stores and servers in restaurants.

It was really hard to find native speakers.... I went out without any special reason to find native-English-speaking conversation partners. I

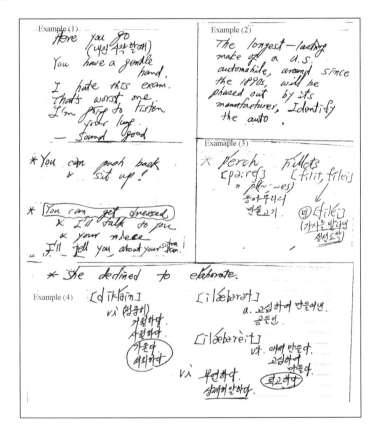

Figure 1.

don't know where I can find native speakers who I can talk to … other than at stores and restaurants.

Sungwoo realized that it was not easy to find opportunities to have conversations with native speakers of English beyond exchanging greetings. He tried to ask many questions in stores and restaurants in order to increase his opportunities to practice English. Soon after, however, he found that spoken skills could not be enhanced much through short conversations with salespersons or waiters in restaurants with whom he exchanged only the same few functional words necessary or only relevant to that situation. As Sungwoo expressed, this lack of contact with native speakers was a big obstacle to learning spoken English through interaction.

In order to get over this social-contextual obstacle to language-learning, Sungwoo tried to find a new workplace where he could work with native speakers of English. After six months of his stay, he was finally able to work in a hospital, observing consulting rooms and operating rooms and working in the hospital research laboratory. In this new workplace, he did have more opportunities to interact with native speakers. However, Sungwoo believed that this increased contact with native speakers was still not enough to improve his spoken English skills.

Influence of insecurity about speaking English in the presence of Koreans on limiting learning opportunities
Sungwoo's insecurity about speaking English in the presence of Koreans was another social-contextual factor that played a role in limiting his opportunity to speak and learn English. He said that he was afraid to make a mistake and tended not to speak English in the presence of other Koreans either in ESL classes that he attended some evenings after work or on other social occasions. This was observed in two sections of the ESL classes he attended. He frequently asked questions in the class where there were no Koreans, whereas he did not ask any questions or speak unless he was called on in a class with other Koreans. When asked why he asked more questions in one class than in the other, he replied,

It is America, but there are many Koreans around me, in the neighborhood, in the workplace, and at church. And we know each other, especially through Korean church…. For example, after I made a mistake in a class where there were other Koreans, I heard from other Koreans that I had made the mistake. I was shocked to hear that…. I felt really insecure about speaking English, especially making mistakes. So I am a little afraid to make mistakes in the class where other Koreans are…. In the presence of other Koreans, I would rather not speak English unless I am sure that I can say it correctly.

This excerpt reveals Sungwoo's insecurity about speaking English in the presence of other Koreans and how it limited his opportunities to speak English. This finding is consistent with Kang's (2005) finding that Koreans tend to feel less secure about making mistakes and more reluctant to speak English in the presence of Koreans than of other international students. These findings can be better understood in relation to other research. According to MacIntyre and Gardner (1989), errors can be a source of anxiety for some individuals because they draw attention to the difficulty of making positive social impressions when speaking a new language. Sungwoo, who perceived himself as a non-fluent English speaker, was very much aware of his difficulty in making a positive social impression when he spoke English. Sungwoo's awareness of this difficulty was an important source of his insecurity about speaking English. Taking into account the Korean concept of face-saving, called *Che-myon* in Korean, Sungwoo's insecurity about speaking English in the presence of other Koreans can be better understood. Because *Che-myon* plays an important role in Koreans' social behavior, Koreans wish to keep *Che-myon*, especially in the presence of other Koreans. Due to *Che-myon*, Koreans are sensitive to other Koreans' negative evaluation of them. For Koreans, especially those living in an English-speaking country, spoken English proficiency can be a principal way of evaluating other Koreans, attributable to their tendency to place a high value on education and intelligence shown in the ability to speak English. When speaking English, as a result, Koreans tend to be seriously concerned about losing their *Che-myon* because other Koreans evaluate them negatively on the basis of their English errors. The role of *Che-myon* in Koreans' English-related social behavior has also been revealed in earlier studies (Park, 1998), which stated that Koreans do not wish their level of English to be judged by their fellow Koreans due to *Che-myon*. This insecurity, which made Sungwoo hesitant to speak English in the presence of other Koreans, along with the lack of contact with native speakers, played a role as social-contextual obstacles limiting his opportunities to speak and to learn English.

Interactions Between Individual and Social-Contextual Factors

Role of extroversion in overcoming insecurity in the presence of Koreans

Sungwoo's extroversion appeared to contribute to overcoming to some degree his insecurity about speaking English in the presence of Koreans, which illustrates the interaction between an individual factor and a social-contextual factor. Sungwoo seemed to overcome the insecurity about speaking English in the presence of Koreans more quickly than other Koreans. After seven months of his stay, Sungwoo said, "I have tried to ignore other Koreans in ESL classes, and I don't care what they think and say about me."

Sungwoo is definitely an extroverted person. His sociability, which has been suggested as an essential feature of extroversion (Eysenck, 1965;

Eysenck & Chan, 1982), was observed and also expressed by him, along with other characteristics of extroversion such as outgoingness, talkativeness, excitement, and activeness. His extroverted personality, along with his awareness of the negative effect of insecurity on his language-learning, seemed to help him overcome it to some degree. Sungwoo said,

> I thought I could not improve my English during my stay in the United States unless I ignored other Koreans. So I decided to ignore them. Another Korean physician who was in my ESL classes scorned my strong desire to learn English by asking me if I think I can learn English perfectly. Instead of answering, I said to him, "Would you do me a favor by not concerning yourself about my English even though my English is poor?" I also told him I didn't think he had anything to lose when I made a mistake in English speaking.... However, I cannot say I do not experience insecurity in the presence of other Koreans at all, although I have gotten better.

Sungwoo was extroverted enough to ask other Koreans not to care about his mistakes in English. In the member check, Sungwoo also admitted that he was an extroverted person and believed his extroversion helped him get over the insecurity in the presence of other Koreans. Although his extroversion played a principal role in overcoming the insecurity, his strong motivation to improve his spoken English also appeared to contribute. It should be noted that he could not completely overcome his insecurity in the presence of Koreans, but that it was reduced by his extroversion and motivation. By overcoming his insecurity to a certain degree, he was able to increase his opportunities to speak English, possibly facilitating language-learning. This finding that extroversion contributed to increasing opportunities to speak lends support to other research (Krashen, 1985; Lightbown & Spada, 1993; Skehan, 1989).

Role of motivation in overcoming the lack of contact with native speakers
Sungwoo's motivation helped him overcome lack of contact with native speakers, which also demonstrates an interaction between an individual factor and a social-contextual factor. When contact with native speakers was unavailable in his first workplace, he made an effort to find another workplace to gain more opportunities to interact with native speakers. His strong motivation to improve his spoken English during his stay in an English-speaking country was the primary reason why he changed his workplace. Sungwoo said,

> What I really want to do here is improve my spoken English. That's my primary goal.... I will do everything I can do here to improve my English.... While I was working at the lab, I was surrounded by nonnative speakers ... many of them were Chinese. When we did not

communicate well in English, we wrote Chinese letters to communicate our intended message. I was really disappointed with the situation.... no native speakers in America ... I felt panic because of my feeling that I would not be able to improve my English at all in this situation.... So I was really desperate to find another workplace where I can interact with native speakers. Here [hospital], I am surrounded by native speakers ... The doctor whose practice I mainly observed is an Indian, but all the other nurses and other doctors are native speakers ... although I don't think it's enough to improve my English.

As expressed in this excerpt, Sunwoo's comments support the relationship between motivation and learners' efforts, which typically results in success in language proficiency and achievement (Gardner, 1985).

Role of extroversion in overcoming the lack of contact with native speakers
Sunwoo's extroversion also appeared to play a role in his attempts to overcome the lack of contact with native speakers. When we visited a winery, I observed Sungwoo asking about wines, demonstrating his effort to practice English. He confessed that the goal of his conversations in the winery was to increase his opportunities to practice English through interactions with native speakers, not to learn more about the wines. According to Sungwoo, he just wished to practice his English speaking skills by asking questions and testing if his English was understood by the interlocutor, even though he did not fully understand the interlocutor's answers.

Sungwoo also attempted to initiate communication with children in his apartment building and asked many questions in stores and restaurants.

Since I cannot find native speakers, I tried to communicate with children in my apartment building, saying "hi" to them.... But after a couple of times, they didn't like to communicate with me anymore.... At stores, I try to ask as many questions as possible, even if I know the answers, just to practice English. At restaurants, I ask waiters about the food on the menu for the same reason.

Adult Koreans often find it difficult to make the efforts that Sungwoo made to practice English. It appears to be even harder to find physicians, who have a high social status in Korea, making such efforts as initiating conversation with children to practice English. Considering this, as Sungwoo admitted, he was able to make these efforts because of his extroverted personality. In so doing, he increased his opportunities to interact with native speakers, which might not be possible for some introverted persons.

This finding is consistent with Krashen's (1985) observation that extroverts would be likely to maximize the contact and quantity of input received, both of which are generally believed to contribute to language development and learning. This finding also in part supports earlier studies

(Ehrman & Oxford, 1990; Wakamoto, 2000) showing the correlation between extroversion and functional practice strategies such as seeking practice opportunities outside class.

In Sungwoo's case, the social-contextual obstacles to language-learning—his insecurity in the presence of other Koreans and the lack of contact with native speakers—could be overcome to some extent by the role of his individual characteristics of extroversion and high motivation. As a result, Sungwoo was able to increase his opportunities to speak and learn English. This finding illustrates interactions between individual factors and social-contextual factors involving his use and learning of ESL.

Conclusion and Implications

This single-case study has demonstrated that a visiting Korean physician's, Sungwoo's, learning and use of ESL were affected by both his individual factors and social-contextual factors, which interacted with each other. Sungwoo's individual characteristics affected his learning and use of ESL:.
- Perfectionist personality influenced his desire to speak correct English;
- Occupation influenced his fear of speaking incorrectly;
- Occupation influenced his desire to speak formally and politely;
- Beliefs about language-learning influenced his use of language-learning strategies.

Social-contextual factors also influenced his learning and use of ESL:
- Lack of contact with native speakers influenced his language-learning, limiting opportunities to speak and learn English;
- Insecurity about speaking English in the presence of other Koreans influenced his language-learning, limiting opportunities to speak and learn English.

Moreover, there were interactions between individual and social-contextual factors.
- Extroversion and motivation played a role in overcoming the insecurity in the presence of Koreans;
- Motivation and extroversion played a role in overcoming the lack of contact with native speakers.

Due to these interactions, he was able to overcome to some degree the social-contextual obstacles limiting his opportunities to speak and learn English.

These findings suggest that an individual's language-learning and use should be understood in relation to both individual and social-contextual factors, and the interaction between these two types of factors should be also considered. These findings also support Abraham and Vann's (1987) and Ellis's (1994) models that suggest that language-learning is affected by both individual and contextual factors, which were addressed by different terms by these researchers and myself: environmental (Abraham & Vann, 1987), situational (Ellis, 1994), and social-contextual factors (this study). The findings of this study differ from the other models, however, in that this study revealed the interaction between the two types of factors.

The findings have useful implications for ESL professionals. The influences of individual factors on language-learning suggest that there should be individualized instruction to increase the effectiveness of instruction and learning (Kang, 2005; Skehan, 1989). ESL professionals should accommodate individual differences in curriculum and teaching practices. Based on the influence of occupation on the fear of speaking incorrectly, for example, ESL professionals teaching physicians should focus more on fluency rather than accuracy in teaching and curriculum and encourage them to take risks in their English speaking. ESL professionals or native-English-speaking interlocutors should avoid frequently correcting errors made by ESL speakers who fear speaking incorrectly like the Korean physician in this study. This is because error corrections may increase their fear of speaking incorrectly and reduce their willingness to communicate (Kang, 2005; MacIntyre, Baker, Clément, & Donovan, 2003; Macintyre, Clément, Dörnyei, & Noels, 1998). Drawing on findings about the influence of social-contextual factors, ESL professionals should inform physicians and other Korean ESL speakers of the existence of the social-contextual obstacles that can be encountered in an English-speaking country and offer recommendations for how to deal with them. As stated by Kang (2003), one of the best ways to overcome lack of contact with native speakers is to develop intercultural friendships. Based on this, ESL professionals may need to include issues regarding L2 speakers' social relationships with native speakers (e.g., how can foreigners develop and maintain intercultural friendships with native speakers?) in their curriculum. ESL professionals' positive social relationships with L2 speakers can contribute to facilitating L2 speakers' positive social relationships with other native speakers, which would increase their opportunities to interact with native speakers.

The fact that the findings of this study were based on a single case should be considered in understanding them. With the findings as a starting point, future studies should investigate more individuals with various characteristics and in various social contexts to support or disconfirm the findings. Future studies may need to examine environmental factors other than social-contextual factors and their influences on language-learning and use. Another direction for future studies is to investigate whether social-contextual environmental factors can facilitate or hamper language-learning beyond the opportunity to speak. Drawing on an understanding of the interactive role of individual and social-contextual factors, future studies should investigate how these two types of factors interact and influence language-learning and use. It is also reasonable to suggest that in the ecological perspective positing the interaction between individual and environmental characteristics (Barton, 1994; Bateson, 1955; Bronfenbrenner, 1979, 1993), future studies examine this interaction more comprehensively.

Acknowledgments

I would like to express my sincere gratitude to the participant, who generously shared his experiences and thoughts for this project, and the reviewers for their helpful comments and suggestions on earlier versions of this article.

The Author

Su-Ja Kang earned a doctorate at SungKyunKwan University in Korea and taught EFL at the university level for seven years. She conducted postdoctoral research in the Department of Linguistics at Harvard University. She is currently a doctoral candidate in foreign/second language education at the University of Buffalo.

References

Abraham, R.G., & Vann, R.J. (1987). Strategies of two language learners: A case study. In A. Wenden & J. Rubin (Eds.), *Learner strategies in language learning* (pp. 85-111). Englewood Cliffs, NY: Prentice-Hall International.

Barton, D. (1994). *Literacy: An introduction to the ecology of written language*. Oxford, UK: Blackwell.

Bateson, G. (1972). *Steps to an ecology of mind*. New York: Ballantine Books.

Bronfenbrenner, U. (1979). *The ecology of human development*. Cambridge, MA: Harvard University Press.

Bronfenbrenner, U. (1993). The ecology of cognitive development: Research models and fugitive findings. In R. Wozniak & K. Fischer (Eds.), *Development in context: Acting and thinking in specific environments* (pp. 3-44). Hillsdale, NJ: Erlbaum.

Butterworth, G., & Hatch, E. (1978). A Spanish-speaking adolescent's acquisition of English syntax. In E. Hatch (Ed.), *Second language acquisition* (pp. 231-245). Rowley, MA: Newbury House.

Brophy, J. (1996). *Teaching problem students*. New York: Guilford Press.

Ellis, R. (1994). *The study of second language acquisition*. Oxford, UK: Oxford University Press.

Ehrman, M.E., Leaver, B.L., & Oxford, R.L. (2003). A brief overview of individual differences in second language learning. *System, 31*, 313-330.

Ehrman, M.E., & Oxford, R.L. (1989). Effects of sex differences, career choice, and psychological type on adults' language learning strategies. *Modern Language Journal, 73*, 1-13.

Ehrman, M.E., & Oxford, R.L. (1990). Adult language learning styles and strategies in an intensive training setting. *Modern Language Journal, 74*, 311-328.

El-Dib, M.A.B. (2004). Language learning strategies in Kuwait: Links to gender, language level, and culture in a hybrid context. *Foreign Language Annals, 37*, 85-95.

Eysenck, H.J. (1965). *Fact and fiction in psychology*. Baltimore, MD: Penguin.

Eysenck, S.B.G., & Chan J. (1982). A comparative study of personality in adults and children: Hong Kong vs. England. *Personality and Individual Differences, 3*, 153-160.

Freed, B.F., Segalowitz, N., & Dewey, D.P. (2004). Context of learning and second language fluency in French: Comparing regular classroom, study abroad, and intensive domestic immersion programs. *Studies in Second language Acquisition, 26*, 275-301.

Gardner, R.C. (1985). *Social psychology and second language learning: The role of attitudes and motivation*. London: Edward Arnold.

Green, J.M., & Oxford, R. (1995). A closer look at learning strategies, L2 proficiency, and gender. *TESOL Quarterly, 29*, 261-297.

Gregersen, T., & Horwitz, E. (2002). Language learning and perfectionism: Anxious and non-anxious language learners' reactions to their own oral performance. *Modern Language Journal, 86*, 562-570.

Harklau, L. (1994). ESL versus mainstream classes: Contrasting L2 learning environments. *TESOL Quarterly, 28*, 241-272.

Jacob, E., Rottenberg, L., Patrick, S., & Wheeler, E. (1996). Cooperative learning: Context and opportunities for acquiring academic English. *TESOL Quarterly, 30*, 253-280.

Jorden, P. (1977). Rules, grammatical intuitions and strategies in foreign language learning. *Interlanguage Studies Bulletin Utrecht, 21*, 25-76.

Kang, S.-J. (2003, May). *Koreans' perceptions of American friends.* Paper presented at the 37th Annual International Convention of Teachers of English to Speakers of Other Languages (TESOL), Baltimore.

Kang, S.-J. (2005) Dynamic emergence of situational willingness to communicate in a second language. *System, 33*, 277-292.

Krashen, S. (1981). Aptitude and attitude in relation to second language acquisition and learning. In K.C. Diller (Ed.), *Individual differences and universals in foreign language aptitude* (pp. 155-175). Rowley, MA: Newbury House.

Krashen, S. (1985). *The input hypothesis.* London: Longman

Lafford, B.A. (2004). The effect of context of learning on the use of communication strategies by learners of Spanish as a second language. *Studies in Second language Acquisition, 26*, 201-225.

Lightbown, P., & Spada N. (1993). *How languages are learned.* Oxford, UK: Oxford University Press.

LoCastro, V. (1994). Learning strategies and learning environments. *TESOL Quarterly, 28*, 409-414.

LoCastro, V. (2001). Individual differences in second language acquisition: Attitudes, learner subjectivity, and L2 pragmatic norms. *System, 29*, 69-89.

MacIntyre, P.D. (1994). Towards a social psychological model of strategy use. *Foreign Language Annals, 27*, 185-195.

MacIntyre, P.D., Baker, S.C., Clément, R., & Donovan, L.A. (2003). Talking in order to learn: willingness to communicate and intensive program. *Canadian Modern Language Review, 59*, 589-607.

MacIntyre, P.D., Clément, R., Dörnyei, Z., & Noels, K.A. (1998). Conceptualizing willingness to communicate in a L2: A situational model of L2 confidence and affiliation. *Modern Language Journal, 82*, 545-562.

MacIntyre, P.D., & Gardner, R.C. (1989). Anxiety and second-language learning: Towards a theoretical clarification. *Language Learning, 39*, 251-275.

Merriam, S.B. (1998). *Qualitative research and case study applications in education.* San Francisco, CA: Jossey-Bass.

Miles, M.B., & Huberman, A.M. (1994). *Qualitative data analysis.* Thousand Oaks, CA: Sage.

Oxford, R.L. (1992). Who are our students?: A synthesis of foreign and second language research on individual differences with implications for instructional practice. *TESL Canada Journal, 9*(2), 30-49.

Oxford, R.L., & Ehrman, M. (1993). Second language research on individual differences. *Annual Review of Applied Linguistics, 13*, 188-205.

Oxford, R.L., & Nyikos, M. (1989). Variables affecting choice of language learning strategies by university students. *Modern Language Journal, 73*, 291-300.

Park, C. (1998). Why not speak English? A study of language use among Korean students in an intensive English program in the United States. *Digital Dissertations.* (UMI No. 9833631)

Politzer, R.L. (1983). Research notes: An exploratory study of self-reported language learning behaviors and their relation to achievement. *Studies in Second Language Acquisition, 6*, 54-68.

Sharkey, J., & Layzer, C. (2000). Whose definition of success? Identifying factors that affect English language learners' access to academic success and resources. *TESOL Quarterly, 34*, 352-368.

Skehan, P. (1989). *Individual differences in second language learning*. London: Arnold.

Skehan, P. (1991). Individual differences in second language learning. *Studies in Second Language Acquisition, 13*, 275-298.

Wakamoto, N. (2000). Language learning strategy and personality variables: Focusing on extroversion and introversion. *IRAL, 38*(1), 71-81.

Yang, N. (1999). The relationship between EFL learners' beliefs and learning strategy use. *System, 27*(4), 515-535.

"Why Didn't They Show Up?" Rethinking ESL Parent Involvement in K-12 Education

Yan Guo

When I visited Canadian elementary and secondary schools over the past 10 years, many teachers told me that it was difficult to get English-as-a-second language (ESL) parents involved in K-12 education. I was often asked by teachers, "Why don't they show up at school?" The absence of ESL parents from school is often misinterpreted as parents' lack of concern about their children's education. However, many ESL parents indicated that they cared passionately. Instead of assuming that ESL parents do not care, educators need to understand the barriers that hinder some parents from participating in their children's education. This article explores the barriers affecting ESL parent-teacher communication based on relevant literature and the author's reflections. It goes on to identify parents' and teachers' varying perspectives on ESL learning, followed by indication of successful strategies to improve ESL parents' participation. The article concludes that schools and teachers must take the initiative if the resource of ESL parent participation is to be fully utilized.

Au cours des dix dernières années, pendant mes visites dans des écoles primaires et secondaires au Canada, plusieurs enseignants m'ont dit qu'il était difficile d'impliquer les parents d'élèves de la maternelle à la 12ᵉ année en ALS dans l'éducation de leurs enfants. Se demandant pourquoi les parents ne venaient pas à l'école, les enseignants se faisaient souvent une idée fausse de l'absence des parents et l'attribuaient à l'indifférence de ceux-ci par rapport à l'éducation de leurs enfants. Plusieurs parents d'enfants en ALS ont indiqué le contraire et ont manifesté un vif intérêt à cet égard. Plutôt de conclure à l'indifférence de ces parents, il faudrait que les enseignants comprennent les obstacles qui empêchent certains parents de participer à l'éducation de leurs enfants. Partant d'une analyse de la documentation pertinente et des réflexions de l'auteur, cet article expose les facteurs qui limitent la communication entre parents et enseignants dans un contexte d'ALS. Il traite également des différentes perspectives des parents et des enseignants sur l'apprentissage en ALS, ainsi que de stratégies éprouvées qui visent une meilleure participation de la part des parents. La conclusion souligne l'importance, pour les écoles et enseignants, de prendre l'initiative et assurer que la ressource que représente la participation des parents soit utilisée à bon escient.

The 2001 Census of Canada (Statistics Canada, 2003) reports that almost 5,335,000 people, about one out of every six in the country, speak languages other than English or French as their mother tongue. The Canadian K-12 English as a Second Language (ESL) population includes considerable numbers of students at risk of educational failure (Gunderson, 2004; Watt & Roessingh, 2001). Watt and Roessingh's Calgary study reports a 74% dropout rate for the ESL high school population, and Gunderson finds that 61% of the ESL high school students in Vancouver disappeared from their academic courses.

There are many reasons why ESL students may experience such a high rate of school failure. One reason is poor home-school communication (Ogbu, 1982; Osborne, 1996). Some research suggests that whereas white parents were increasing participation in their children's education, ESL parents' contacts with their children's schools were actually decreasing (Moles, 1993). Over the years, research has also repeatedly revealed that limited communication between ESL parents and teachers has been a serious problem confronting educators (Naylor, 1994; Gougeon, 1993; Salzberg, 1998; Yao, 1988); in fact, the Alberta Beginning Teachers' Survey (Malatest & Associates, 2003) indicates that the difficulties beginning teachers have in communicating with ESL parents[1] also plague many experienced teachers (Faltis, 1997).

In the past 10 years when I visited Canadian elementary and secondary schools, many teachers told me that it was difficult to get ESL parents involved in K-12 education. I have often been asked by teachers "Why don't they show up at school?" This article is an attempt to explore various barriers that affect ESL parent-teacher communication based on relevant literature and my reflections followed by an overview of successful strategies to improve ESL parent participation. It concludes that schools and teachers must take the initiative if the resource of ESL parent participation is to be fully utilized.

ESL parents' involvement in the public schools presents a significant challenge (Moles, 1993). For example, Cumming (1995), in his *Review of ESL Services in the Vancouver School Board*, comments,

> The VSB has translated numerous relevant documents into a wide variety of languages, which are clearly displayed and readily available at VSB offices and at the Oakridge Reception and Orientation Centre. But problems of communicating with ESL students' parents and families on an ongoing basis, after initial stages of students' receptions into the VSB, seem acute and need to be addressed programmatically. (p. 90)

The relationship a school has with ESL parents needs to be seen in the wider context of the international community. For example, the Calderdale decision was formulated in the United Kingdom in the 1980s (Leung & Franson, 2001) after a group of ESL parents successfully sued a school authority because they felt that their children were being "ghettoized" in an ESL program. On the basis of this decision, the Ministry of Education prohibited ESL programs throughout the UK, and ESL teachers now work as support teachers in content classes. In the United States, California Proposition 227, known as the Unz Initiative (Crawford, 1997), passed with a 61% approval in 1998 and eliminated all forms of ESL instruction and bilingual programs in that state except a one-year sheltered English immersion. As in the UK, the dissatisfaction and misunderstanding of some of those closely associated with these programs were factors here too, with large numbers of Hispanic parents voting against ESL and bilingual education. Parents believed that their children were not learning English quickly enough. The message from this is clear: Even if most parents are satisfied with ESL programs, it is important to reach smaller groups who are not satisfied and may not fully understand the program. It is important for educators to listen to ESL parents. And the two examples above reveal another mechanism as well: politicians can take ESL parents' dissatisfaction as an excuse to cut ESL funding. As a result, ESL students may not get the support that they need.

The issue of communication between schools and ESL parents has moved to the foreground recently. In British Columbia, the Vancouver and Richmond School Boards have both been approached with proposals for traditional schools, with claims of support from ESL parents (*Globe and Mail*, February 1, 1999). Most of the parents involved are recent Chinese immigrants who are unhappy with the work their children are doing in Vancouver and Richmond public schools; they have also expressed endorsement of "teacher-led instruction, a homework policy, dress code or uniforms, regular study and conduct reports, frequent meetings between parents and teachers, and additional extra-curricular activities" (Sullivan, 1998, p. 15). It is worth noting that this debate has been presented as being between two familiar sides, the traditional and the progressive, a contrast that does not always fit local conditions. There is a danger that the ready-made rhetoric of the public debate may turn attention away from classroom realities and that calls for simplistic solutions may distract attention from valuable educational approaches to real needs. In the Richmond School District, difficulties of communication with Chinese Canadian parents have become a major political question (Gaskell, 2001). Yet communication between schools and ESL parents is a relatively neglected research area despite the fact that miscommunication has the potential to derail the provision of multicultural and minority education.

Barriers to ESL Parent Involvement

Teacher-parent communication is fraught with complexity for a variety of reasons. Communicating with parents whose first language is not English and whose children are struggling academically highlights the difficulty of home-school interactions in a context of not only linguistic but also cultural differences between immigrant parents and Canadian teachers. Research suggests that many teachers have little idea about how to work effectively with parents from different cultural backgrounds (Malatest & Associates, 2003; Griego Jones, 2003; Mujawamariya & Mahrouse, 2004). In these circumstances, establishment of fruitful parent-teacher communication seems to be challenged by a number of potential barriers, which can be divided into five main categories: language differences, parent unfamiliarity with the school system, teacher attitudes and institutional racism, different views of education, and cultural differences concerning home-school communication.

For ESL parents, language is the major barrier to communicating with teachers. The British Columbia Teachers' Federation reports that many parents of ESL students try to communicate with schools, but are hampered by their English ability and the lack of available translation services (Naylor, 1993b). As Scarcella (1990) explains, "frequently, [ESL] parents avoid going to schools because they cannot communicate in English, and there is no one at school who speaks their native language" (p. 162).

Reciprocally, the school system shows its lack of commitment to ESL parents by predominantly using English in most formal school-parent communication. Gougeon (1993) reports that ESL parents often depend on their children to interpret mail, answer the telephone, translate newsletters, and interpret at parent-teacher conferences. But asking ESL students to act as translators may be problematic, as they are learning English themselves; their language skills may prevent them from understanding the subtleties of coded speech in the school context. Sometimes ESL students may not translate the authentic message. For example, Meza, one of my student teachers reported that he witnessed a Spanish-speaking ESL student deliberately translating the wrong message to his parents when his teacher complained about his behavior problem (Meza, personal communication, 2005). Using a student to translate for the parent in this case creates miscommunication between the teacher and the parent. Finally, the use of educational jargon can also hinder effective parent-teacher communication; although some ESL parents are bilingual, they may not have mastered the particular language of education (Gaskell, 2001).

Unfamiliarity with the school system of the host country is another barrier that prevents some ESL parents from participating in school activities (Delgado-Gaitan, 1990; Gibson, 1987). In her study of Punjabi students' academic achievement in a US high school, Gibson reports that many parents in that particular setting had little understanding of the US system of education, and few were able to help with homework or course selection. Like Gibson, Delgado-Gaitan's examination of the family life of Mexican children in the US also found that many parents in the study were unable to offer their children academic advice because they were unacquainted with the school system.

Regrettably, many teachers misunderstand the lack of parent involvement as indicating a lack of interest and concern about what the children are studying (Delgado-Gaitan, 1990). ESL parents' absence from school is often misinterpreted as parents not caring about their children's education. However, many ESL parents indicate that they care passionately (Cline & Necochea, 2001; Griego Jones, 2003). Instead of assuming that ESL parents do not care, educators need to understand the barriers that hinder some parents from participating in their children's education. Educators also need to examine their own biases toward ESL parents. Research suggests that many teachers often do not have sufficiently high expectations for ESL students and parents (Griego Jones, 2003; Ramirez, 2003). Ramirez reports that many Latino immigrant parents in a predominantly Latino community in California felt that teachers have low expectations for their students. They complained that teachers had an inbuilt assumption of Latino parents' inferiority. They believed that the schools did not listen or care to listen to their needs as parents.

Teachers' attitudes toward parents and their efforts to involve parents are critical to parents' participation and to school effectiveness. In addition to some teachers' attitudes and racial biases toward immigrant parents, institutional racism is another major hurdle that can prevent immigrant parents from participating in school activities. Cline and Necochea (2001) suggest,

> The quest for parental involvement comes with a caveat—only parental involvement that is supportive of school policies and instructional practices is welcome here ... parents whose culture, ethnicity, SES, and language background differ drastically from the white middle-class norms are usually kept at a distance, for their views, values, and behaviors seem "foreign" and strange to traditional school personnel. (p. 23)

Their study shows how institutional racism can exclude immigrant parents from involvement opportunities. Cline and Necochea report that a group of Latino parents in the Lompoc Unified School District in California wanted a bilingual program for their children, but their request was dismissed by their children's school and the school district. These parents were not allowed to meet with the teachers of their children; they were perceived as difficult, stupid, and selfish. Many Latino parents in that particular setting also complained that their children were treated unfairly as a result of social and institutional racism. However, the district administrators attempted to silence them. It will be difficult for schools to expect immigrant parents to participate in school activities if they are not welcome and their voices are not heard. Moreover, class and race may also play a role in parent-school interaction. Lareau (2003) found that White and Black middle-class parents were more strategic in intervening at school than Black working-class parents were. Both middle- and working-class Black parents were continually concerned with schools' racial discrimination. In this regard, it is worth noting that Canadian or US models of parent involvement have tended to focus more on middle-class than-working class values and concerns and on experiences more relevant to parents of Anglo-Celtic descent than to those from non-English-speaking backgrounds or of Aboriginal descent. The importance of non-dominant forms of parent involvement from various races and social classes has been overlooked.

In addition, there is evidence that some teachers may actually discourage ESL parents' participation in school curricular activities (Cummins, 1986). These teachers believe that parents' first-language interaction with their children interferes with second-language learning. This belief has been refuted by many scholars (Coelho, 2004; Cummins, 2005). However, during my visits to Canadian schools, many teachers still strongly hold such a belief. For example, some teachers advised their ESL parents: "You should stop speaking your native languages at home so that your children can learn English." Despite the fact that English is a language in which many parents are not easily able to express themselves, these teachers advise ESL parents to speak English at home in order to help their children. As Scarcella (1990) explains, "when ESL parents switch to English, they often deprive their children of exposure to valuable input in their first language, eradicate their children's cultural identities, and expose their children to an imperfect variety of English" (p. 164). There is no empirical evidence to support the claim that English is best taught monolingually. Educators must abolish the damaging view that stamping out immigrant students' languages will somehow ensure educational success. They need to recognize students' first languages as an important component of their identity, a useful tool for thinking and learning, and a valuable medium for effective communication in the family and the community.

Another major obstacle to developing educational partnerships with ESL parents can be teachers' and parents' differing views of education. It is beyond the scope of this article to discuss each cultural group; however, the numbers of Chinese[2] immigrants in Canada—the largest visible minority group, reaching 1,029,400 in 2001 (Statistics Canada, 2003)—warrant a closer examination of their assumptions about education. Ghuman and Wong (1989) interviewed 34 Chinese families in Manchester, UK. They found that Chinese parents valued education highly, wanted more homework for their children, and preferred a stricter regime in schools. They interpreted the self-discipline and informality in British schools as being lax and ineffective. The researchers also found that students' perceived lack of respect for teachers in the British education system was a concern for parents rooted in their own cultural norms.

Salzberg (1998) conducted ethnographic interviews with eight Taiwanese ESL families in Vancouver. Her findings show that parents were not satisfied with the holistic learner-centered approaches prevalent in Canadian schools. They also expressed discomfort with the long periods (most students took two to three years) spent in non-credit ESL classes without clear criteria for advancement. Parents were anxious to mainstream their children, as they believed second-language learning was delayed through separate ESL classes. Parents also considered ESL classes as preventing students from learning content-area material. These Taiwanese ESL parents tended to prefer greater use of testing, more intensive homework tied to material that was more frequently tested, and teachers functioning as disciplinarians, urging students to greater academic progress as measured by such tests.

As discussed above, Chinese ESL parents have high expectations with respect to their children's education; yet many voice mixed feelings or even frustrations in their perceptions of their children's ESL programs. How do ESL teachers perceive ESL parents' concerns? Gougeon (1993) conducted interviews with 27 teachers in one school in Alberta. He found that from the teachers' point of view, Chinese parents were distrustful of the Canadian school system: the lack of national entrance exams, and the absence of student discipline. Also, they were confused about the significance of credentials and about the Canadian style of teaching and learning. According to one teacher, "I think they [ESL parents] may feel very disappointed with the Canadian system. They do not view this as real learning" (p. 265). Gougeon's data analysis shows that the teachers were aware that many ESL parents criticized the laxity of the host country school system in general and of teaching styles in particular.

Communication between ESL parents and teachers can be problematic. On the one hand, many ESL parents view ESL learning as not real learning (Ghuman & Wong, 1989; Gougeon 1993; Guo, 2002; Salzberg, 1998). On the other hand, many teachers regard learning English as crucial for ESL students before they move to mainstream classes. Guo's study of an ESL program in Canadian schools shows that teachers believed that ESL programs helped ESL students acquire proficiency in the four language skills of listening, speaking, reading, and writing within the shortest possible time. Teachers also believed that ESL classes helped students to acquire basic study skills and to be socialized into North American school culture, which they believed were fundamental to their continued education in Canada. Moreover, many authoritative texts on ESL teaching and learning advocate teaching methodologies that promote critical thinking, reflective teaching, communicative teaching methods, the integration of language and content, and cooperative learning (Brown, 2000; Snow & Brinton, 1997), and ESL teachers are encouraged to use interactive techniques, group or individual self-evaluations, and learner-centered activities (Brown).

Teachers and ESL parents are deeply divided on both what and how students should learn, and schools do not always seem to value ESL parents' views of education (Guo, 2002). Guo finds that both Canadian teachers and immigrant parents have the same aims: providing the best education for immigrant students. However, as Delpit (1988) asserts, parents who do not function in the culture of power often want their children to learn the code of power. The above studies indicate that Chinese ESL parents want direct, intentional, and individual language instruction for their children; lack of attention to this concern has created dissatisfaction among many Chinese immigrant parents.

A further barrier to ESL parent involvement in schools is cultural differences concerning home-school communication. Communicating with schools as one type of parent involvement is the norm in North America. Parents are expected to come to routine parent-teacher conferences before or after they receive their child's report card. They are also expected to volunteer at school functions, help their children with their homework, and initiate parent-teacher meetings if they have any particular concerns (Delgado-Gaitan, 1990). However, parent involvement is mainly a North American concept; it is neither expected nor practiced in China (Ogbu, 1995). ESL parents from a focus group discussion conducted by the British Columbia Teachers' Federation reported that "the notion of helping in schools is a 'western idea,' so they need more outreach to involve them" (Naylor, 1993a, p. 2). In fact, parents' presence in schools may have negative associations; Chan (1976) explains that in Hong Kong, Chinese parents seldom attend school functions because if the school asks to see parents, it means their children have got into trouble. This social stigma associated with communicating with teachers might prevent some Chinese ESL parents from interacting with schools when they come to Canada.

Other researchers find Asian parents are reluctant to challenge a teacher's authority because in their cultures teachers are held in high esteem. Scarcella (1990) notes, for example, that

> recalling the traditional Vietnamese respect and awe with which the teacher is regarded, one realises that the teacher can expect the total support of the parents. Learning is highly valued, and teachers are ranked just below the king and above the father. (p. 167)

Asian parents see teachers as professionals with authority over their children's schooling. They believe that parents should not interfere with school processes. Yao (1988) explains that Asian parents usually do not initiate contact with schools, as they see communication with teachers as a culturally disrespectful way of monitoring them.

Most ESL parents believe that they are responsible for nurturing and educating their children at home, not at school. For example, Espinosa (1995) explains,

> throughout Hispanic culture there is a widespread belief in the absolute authority of the school and teachers. In many Latin American countries it is considered rude for a parent to intrude into the life of the school. Parents believe that it is the school's job to educate and the parent's job to nurture and that the two jobs do not mix. A child who is well educated is one who has learned moral and ethical behavior.

Of course, there is a danger of overgeneralizing about ESL parents, who in reality are a diverse group with complex needs and expectations, but at the same time, it is helpful for teachers to learn about immigrant cultures in order to communicate with immigrant parents effectively. It is also important to keep in mind that teachers should learn and value parents' individual personalities and differences in a particular culture and across cultures.

If parent involvement is not the norm for Chinese parents, how do they communicate with schools? Chinese parents are in fact very much involved in their children's education. In China, parents get plenty of information about their children's education. Parents know their children's progress through looking at their textbooks, daily homework assignments, and the scores of frequent tests (Li, 2002). Chyu and Smith (1991) note how parents of high school students in Taiwan are required to sign the homework booklet before the child returns it to the school. It is generally

> the duty of the individual teacher or school guidance counselor to contact or call parents in case of minor student-related problems. Parents-teacher conferences are rare, and parents assume all is well if their child does not request that the parent see a teacher. (p. 133)

More recently, in some schools in Taiwan, teachers keep contact with parents through electronic mail (T. Yang, personal communication, 2001). A class list server is built for parents of children who are in the same class. The *daoshi* (homeroom teacher) posts daily homework assignments to the class list server so that every parent receives them. The teacher also informs specific parents about individual behavior and other problems. If parents have a question or concern, they can also contact the teacher via electronic mail. In Canada, Chinese parents reported that they supported their children's efforts by providing a print-rich home environment and quiet study areas and by taking their children to the public library (Li, 2002). One parent reported that she sat down with her children when they did their homework to affirm the value she placed on their education, even though she could not help them with their work (Guo, 2002). This example demonstrates that even though this parent may not be able to show up at the school for school activities, sitting with her children when they were doing their homework signals that she cares about her children's education. This example also shows that even though this type of activity is not a typical parent involvement recognized by Canadian teachers, it is a unique way for this Chinese immigrant parent to help her children's education.

The existing literature on ESL home-school relations has centered on the barriers that hinder smooth communication between teachers and ESL parents with little emphasis on the conditions required for a real dialogue among diverse voices. What can help teachers and ESL parents communicate better with each other? Is it possible to conduct a real dialogue about their differing views of education? I address some of the conditions needed for building partnership with ESL parents in the following sections.

Implications for Successful ESL Parent Involvement

Although a school may be unable to address all the barriers to ESL parent-teacher communication, there are many steps that schools can take that will assist in increasing parent participation. This part of the article addresses mainly the needs of Chinese-speaking parents; I do not claim that all strategies mentioned in relation to Chinese-speaking parents would work for any ESL parent. However, educators can still learn from these strategies and apply them judiciously in their own contexts. The first step is to deal with language issues. For example, for schools serving significant populations of Chinese-speaking parents, it is important that all communication should be bilingual. Schools should provide interpreters for parent-teacher meetings instead of using students to translate for their parents.

Bilingual staff can not only provide translation, but also act as intermediaries between ESL parents and teachers. In their study of Chinese parental involvement in the schooling process, Constantino, Cui, and Faltis (1995) report that the active intervention of third parties, such as Chinese bilingual resource teachers, serving as a bridge between teachers and parents determined the success of parent-teacher communication. Their study indicates that parents and teachers placed different weight on parent-teacher meetings. Teachers believed that all parents should attend the meetings. In contrast, parents chose not to attend because in addition to language barriers, they did not understand the significance placed on the meetings. As a response to this problem, the Chinese bilingual resource teacher attached Chinese translations to all the signs in the school area and translated many school forms and the monthly school newsletter. The resource teacher also offered teachers discussions about Asian and Chinese culture, cultural values, and the myriad roles members play in that culture, as well as a crash course in conversational Chinese. Because of these active interventions, teachers and Chinese ESL parents were more at ease when they communicated with each other, and more Chinese parents attended meetings with teachers.

Another effort schools can make is to help ESL parents understand the school system. One way to do this is to organize parents' nights. In a study of parents' nights organized by a Canadian secondary school (Guo, 2002), parents said that they were useful in providing them with general information about school policies and the ESL program. In this ESL program, students normally studied noncredit modified-content subjects such as ESL social studies and ESL science for two years, along with credit math and physical education in mainstream classes. For example, at one parents' night, the teachers addressed the following questions: (a) What do we do in our ESL classes? (b) How do students move from ESL into mainstream classes? (c) How can parents help their children in ESL classes? (d) What are some of the problems ESL students have when they reach mainstream classes? and (e) What are our expectations regarding homework? Guo shows parents' nights were effective as an educational event for newly arrived ESL parents. The sessions had good attendance, and a number of the parents who attended expressed their appreciation.

Another step toward increasing ESL parent participation is for schools to ask teachers to examine their own feelings, understandings, and biases toward ESL parents (Griego Jones, 2003; Ramirez, 2003). A school district can also offer professional development workshops on cultural sensitivity to help inservice teachers deal with their attitudes. It is important for teachers to learn what obstacles to school involvement ESL parents face and what they can do to overcome these obstacles. One thing teachers can do is to move beyond the *holiday approach* (Naylor, 1993a) and the *multicultural food approach*, which are popular teacher practices to involve ESL parents. When I asked teachers what they did to promote ESL parent involvement, many told me that they invited ESL parents to celebrate holidays from different cultures. They asked their students to dress in their ethnic clothes. Other school principals told me they organized a multicultural dinner annually and they were happy because many ESL parents became involved. However, educators should move beyond ethnic foods, dress, and festivities when trying to involve ESL parents. As MacPherson et al. (2004) suggest, educators need to invite ESL parents to "participate in all decision-making, but especially decision-making about multicultural, ESL, Aboriginal, and/or heritage language maintenance programs in schools" (p. 16). Teachers can also foster two-way communication by not only providing information to parents, but also listening to parents' input. Constantino (1994) reports that one ESL secondary instructor adopted several approaches to increase parental involvement. For example, the teacher used an ESL Parent Teacher Association in which the parents chose the topics for discussion, ranging from preventing children from joining gangs to what the students needed to study every night. She also sent home a monthly newsletter and calendar to inform parents of her students' school activities.

Schools must address better the needs of a multicultural, multilingual population. Mohan et al. (1996) suggest that educators and administrators need to recognize that educational tasks may be open to culturally divergent interpretations; that is, teachers, students, and parents may have culturally different views of the educational agenda. Schools, therefore, need to become learning organizations "where people continually expand their capacity to create the results they truly desire, where new and expansive patterns of thinking are nurtured, where collective aspiration is set free, and where people are continually learning how to learn together" (Senge, 1990, p. 3).

Learning together with ESL parents is an important task for teachers in multilingual and multicultural schools. Gunderson (2001) notes that "North American educators continue to view education within a 'mainstream' viewpoint, one that focuses on European values and beliefs, even though their school population grows increasing multicultural" (p. 247). Specifically, Ovando and McLaren (1999) posit that minority students are disadvantaged by school culture, curriculum, teaching methodology, and assessment measures that serve the Euro-North American middle-class norm. Schools and districts need to recognize that it is crucial to adapt the educational system to reflect its multicultural and multilingual community. One option is to incorporate ESL parents' home cultures into the school curriculum (Dyson, 2001). For example, parents may visit the classroom to share their knowledge, or students may be given homework assignments that require that they interview their parents or their grandparents about their communities or their immigration experiences (Gonzalez et al., 1993). This kind of activity helps to acknowledge parents' cultural values by showing them that they can provide valuable contributions. This also helps students make better connections between the school curriculum and their personal experiences, which in turn will help students succeed academically.

Another strategy in adapting the educational system is to acknowledge the unique ways that ESL parents are involved in their children's education. For example, Lopez (2001) studied a Mexican migrant family, the Padillas, in Texas; all five of the children had graduated from high school in the top 10% of their classes. His findings led him to propose an expansion of traditional parent involvement. The Padillas did not participate in such conventional forms of parent involvement as bake sales, fundraisers, the Parent Teacher Association, or back-to-school nights. Nor did they volunteer in school, attend school activities, or participate on parent advisory councils and/or school governance boards. Such types of parent involvement emphasize the norm of middle-class status. Instead, the Padillas took their children to work with them in the fields and helped them realize that without an education they might end up working in similar jobs. By doing so, the Padillas gave their children a choice: either work hard at school or work hard in the fields. They understood involvement in the sense of teaching "their children to appreciate the value of their education through the medium of hard work" (p. 420). Lopez argues that the "transmission of sociocultural values" (p. 430) is also a type of parent involvement. Educators need to move beyond using participation at school events as the only indicator of ESL parent involvement so as to recognize the full range of ESL parents' contributions to their children's education.

Teacher education programs should increase their efforts to prepare teachers to involve ESL parents (Griego Jones, 2003; MacPherson et al., 2004). Gordon (1994) details a model that could add not only more students of color to the teaching force, but also produce teachers better trained to work with a diverse student population. Also, these programs should include information about the important role of the home in minority students' academic success. Student teachers should learn about the needs of ESL parents and become aware of their own and the parents' cultural assumptions about education. Monolingual teachers also need to be challenged to understand what it feels like to be an ESL student (Kubota, Gardner, Patten, Thatcher-Fettig, & Yoshida, 2000). I recently used a language shock activity to introduce the ESL method of Total Physical Response in a teacher education program. The students were asked to follow my directions in Chinese. They were also asked to observe their classmates' physical reactions and share their emotional responses at the end of the activity. Some of them became frustrated and asked me if I could speak English. This language shock activity provided an opportunity for the student teachers to experience first hand what it was like to be an ESL student. I also hoped that they would become more sensitive when later addressing the affective needs of their own ESL students. As MacPherson et al. (2004) suggest, teachers need to develop the intercultural ability to move "across cultures in a way that is tolerant of conflicting perspectives and deeply respectful of people's lived differences" (p. 5). This intercultural ability requires that teachers move beyond learning about other groups to reach the stage of examining the cultural contexts that have influenced their own behavior, attitudes, and beliefs (Mujawamariya & Mahrouse, 2004; Solomon & Levine-Rasky, 2003).

Conclusion

It is critical for schools to adopt successful approaches to working with ESL parents because schools and parents alike share the goal of providing the best education for ESL students. Many ESL parents do in fact participate in the education of their children, but in ways that are not always recognized and valued by teachers. Existing research centers primarily on helping parents to learn about schools. Further research is needed on how teachers can learn more about ESL families and how they may develop increased intercultural ability: educators often focus on what is lacking in ESL families rather than on the potential resources on which they can build. Schools and teachers must take the initiative if the resource of ESL parent participation is to be fully utilized. The work of achieving social justice must involve ESL parents, and ESL parents' voices must be heard.

Notes

[1]The term *ESL parents* in this article refers to parents of children who speak English as a second language and who are schooled in ESL and mainstream classes.

[2]This is not to say that the Chinese are a homogeneous cultural group. In fact there are significant differences in the political, economic, social, and educational systems between China and Taiwan. Thus caution in generalizations about Chinese parents is needed.

The Author

Yan Guo is an assistant professor in the TESL Program of the Faculty of Education, University of Calgary. She teaches courses in second-language acquisition, second-language reading and writing, and ESL mythology. Her research interests include intercultural communication, ESL parent involvement, second-language writing, second-language acquisition and identity, and content-based ESL learning.

References

Brown, D.H. (2000). *Teaching by principles: An interactive approach to language pedagogy* (2nd ed.). Englewood Cliffs, NJ: Prentice Hall.

Chan, I. (1976). The Chinese immigrant: Language and cultural concerns. *TESL Talk, 7,* 9-19.

Chyu, L., & Smith, D. (1991). Secondary academic education. In D.C. Smith (Ed.), *The Confucian continuum: Educational modernization in Taiwan* (pp. 99-165). New York: Praeger.

Cline, Z., & Necochea, J. (2001). ¡Basta Ya! Latino parents fighting entrenched racism. *Bilingual Research Journal, 25,* 1-26.

Coelho, E. (2004). *Adding English: A guide to teaching in multilingual classrooms.* Toronto, ON: Pippin.

Constantino, R. (1994). A study concerning instruction of ESL students comparing all-English classroom teacher knowledge and English as a second language teacher knowledge. *Journal of Educational Issues of Language Minority Students, 13,* 37-57.

Constantino, R., Cui, L., & Faltis, C. (1995). Chinese parental involvement: Reaching new levels. *Equity and Excellence in Education, 28,* 46-50.

Crawford, J. (1997). The campaign against proposition 227: A post mortem. *Bilingual Research Journal, 21,* 1-29.

Cumming, A. (1995). *A review of ESL services in the Vancouver School Board.* Toronto, ON: Ontario Institute for Studies in Education.

Cummins, J. (1986). Empowering minority students: A framework for intervention. *Harvard Educational Review, 56,* 18-36.

Cummins, J. (2005). *Challenging monolingual instructional assumptions in second language immersion and bilingual program.* Paper presented at the annual meeting of the American Educational Research Association (AERA), Montreal.

Delgado-Gaitan, C. (1990). *Literacy for empowerment: The role of parents in children's education.* New York: Falmer Press.

Delpit, L. (1988). The silenced dialogue: Power and pedagogy in educating other people's children. *Harvard Educational Review, 58,* 280-298.

Dyson, L. (2001). Home-school communication and expectations of recent Chinese immigrants. *Canadian Journal of Education, 26*, 455-476.

Espinosa, L. (1995). Hispanic parent involvement in early childhood programs. *ERIC Digest EDO-PS-95-3*. Retrieved April 2, 2004, from http://ceep.crc.uiuc.edu/eecearchive/digests/1995/espino95.html

Faltis, C. (1997). *Joinfostering: Adapting teaching for the multicultural classroom* (2nd ed.). Upper Saddle River, NJ: Prentice Hall.

Gaskell, J. (2001). The "public" in public schools: A school board debate. *Canadian Journal of Education, 26*, 19-36.

Ghuman, P., & Wong, R. (1989). Chinese parents and English education. *Educational Research, 31*, 134-140.

Gibson, M. (1987). Punjabi immigrants in an American high school. In G. Spindler & L. Spindler (Eds.), *Interpretive ethnography of education: At home and abroad* (pp. 281-310). Hillsdale, NJ: Erlbaum.

Gonzalez, N., Moll, L.C., Floyd-Tenery, M., Rivera, A., Rendon, P., Gonzales, R., & Amanti, C. (1993). *Teacher research on funds of knowledge: Learning from households*. Educational Practice Report No. 6. Santa Cruz, CA; Washington, DC: National Center for Research on Cultural Diversity and Second Language Learning.

Gordon, J. (1994). Preparing future teachers of diversity. *Urban Review, 26*, 25-35.

Gougeon, T. (1993). Urban schools and immigrant families: Teacher perspectives. *Urban Review, 25*, 251-287.

Griego Jones, T. (2003). Contributions of Hispanic parents' perspectives to teacher preparation. *School Community Journal*, 73-96.

Gunderson, L. (2001). Different cultural views of whole language. In S. Boran & B. Comber (Eds.), *Critiquing whole language and classroom inquiry* (pp. 242-271). Urbana, IL: National Council of Teachers of English.

Gunderson, L. (2004). The language, literacy, achievement, and social consequences of English-only programs for immigrant students. In J. Hoffman, D. Schallert, B. Maloch, J. Worth, & C. Fairbanks (Eds.), *The 53rd yearbook of the National Reading Conference* (pp. 1-33). Milwaukee, MI: National Reading Conference.

Guo, Y. (2002). *Chinese parents and ESL teachers: Understanding and negotiating their differences*. Unpublished doctoral dissertation. University of British Columbia.

Kubota, R., Gardner, K., Patten, M., Thatcher-Fettig, C., & Yoshida, M. (2000). Mainstream peers try on English language learners' shoes: A shock language experience. *TESOL Journal, 9*, 12-16.

Lareau, A. (2003). *Unequal childhoods: Class, race, and family life*. Berkeley, CA: University of California Press.

Leung, C., & Franson, C. (2001). England: ESL in the early days. In B. Mohan, C. Leung, & C. Davison (Eds.), *English as a second language in the mainstream* (pp. 153-164). Harlow, UK: Pearson Education.

Li, G. (2002). *"East is east, west is west?" Home literacy, culture, and schooling*. New York: Peter Lang.

Lopez, G.R. (2001). The value of hard work: Lessons on parent involvement from an (im)migrant household. *Harvard Educational Review, 71*, 416-437.

MacPherson, S., Turner, D., Khan, R., Hingley, W., Tigchelarr, A., & Lafond, L.D. (2004). ESL and Canadian multiculturalism: Multilingual, intercultural practices for the 21st century. *TESL Canada Journal, special issue 4*, 1-22.

Malatest, R.A., & Associates Ltd. (2003). *Efficacy of Alberta teacher preparation programs and beginning teachers' professional development opportunities, 2002 survey report*. Unpublished manuscript. Edmonton, AB: Alberta Learning.

Mohan, B., Early, M., Huxur-Beckett, G., Liang, X., Guo, Y., & Salzberg, J.L. (1996). *The high school community as a learning organization.* Paper presented at annual meeting of Teachers of English to Speakers of Other Language, Chicago.

Moles, O.C. (1993). Collaboration between schools and disadvantaged parents: Obstacles and openings. In N.F. Chavkin (Ed.), *Families and schools in a pluralist society* (pp. 21-49). Albany, NY: SUNY Press.

Mujawamariya, D., & Mahrouse, G. (2004). Multicultural education in Canadian preservice programs: Teacher candidates' perspective. *Alberta Journal of Educational Research, 50,* 336-353.

Naylor, C. (1993a). *The views of parents of ESL students concerning the B.C. education system.* Vancouver, BC: British Columbia Teachers' Federation. Retrieved April 4, 2004, from: http://www.bctf.bc.ca/ResearchReports/93esl06/

Naylor, C. (1993b). *ESL/ESD teachers' focus group responses.* Vancouver, BC: British Columbia Teachers' Federation. Retrieved April 4, 2004, from: http://www.bctf.ca/ResearchReports/93esl05/

Naylor, C. (1994). *A report of the BCTF ESL colloquium.* Vancouver, BC: British Columbia Teachers' Federation. Retrieved April 4, 2004, from: http://www.bctf.bc.ca/ResearchReports/94esl04/

Ogbu, J. (1982) Cultural discontinuities and schooling. *Anthropology and Education Quarterly, 13,* 290-307.

Ogbu, J. (1995). Cultural problems in minority education: Their interpretations and consequences—Part two: Case studies. *Urban Review, 27,* 271-297.

Osborne, A.B. (1996). Practice into theory into practice: Culturally relevant pedagogy for students we have marginalized and normalized. *Anthropology and Education Quarterly, 27,* 285-314.

Ovando, C. & McLaren, P. (Eds.). (1999). *The politics of multiculturalism and bilingual education: Students and teachers caught in the cross fire.* Boston, MA: McGraw-Hill.

Ramirez, A.Y. (2003). Dismay and disappointment: Parental involvement of Latino immigrant parents. *Urban Review, 35,* 93-110.

Salzberg, J. (1998). *Taiwanese immigrant parents' perceptions of their adolescent children's ESL learning and academic achievement.* Unpublished master's thesis. University of British Columbia.

Scarcella, R. (1990). *Teaching language minority students in the multicultural classroom.* Englewood Cliffs, NJ: Prentice-Hall.

Senge, P. (1990). *The fifth discipline: The art and practice of the learning organization.* New York: Doubleday Currency.

Snow, M.A., & Brinton, D. (1997). Introduction. In M.A. Snow & D.M. Brinton (Eds.), *The content-based classroom: Perspectives on integrating language and content* (pp. xi-xiii). White Plains, NY: Addison Wesley Longman.

Solomon, R.P., & Levine-Rasky, C. (2003). *Teaching for equity and diversity: Research to practice.* Toronto, ON: Canadian Scholars' Press.

Statistics Canada. (2003). *Census 2001: Analysis series.* Ottawa: Author.

Sullivan, A. (1998). Chinese lead traditional school drive. *Vancouver Courier, 15.*

Watt, D., & Roessingh, H. (2001). The dynamics of ESL drop-out: Plus a change … *Canadian Modern Language Review, 58,* 203-222.

Yao, E. (1988). Working effectively with Asian immigrant parents. *Phi Delta Kappan, 70,* 223-225.

Feedback on Writing: Changing EFL Students' Attitudes

JoEllen M. Simpson

Extensive research has been conducted about feedback on writing in both L1 and L2 classrooms. Although much of the research suggests that correcting grammar does not help students make long-term improvements, many teachers continue to believe that they must correct all errors. In addition, students report that they want teachers to mark errors. This article reports on the attitude of students of English as a foreign language when presented with feedback that that gives motivating, positive comments coupled with suggestions for improvement. Many students learned to accept this feedback, but many wanted the addition of correction of every grammatical error.

Des recherches approfondies ont porté sur le fait de fournir de la rétroaction sur la rédaction dans les salles de classe L1 et L2. Bien qu'une part importante de la recherche indique que la correction de la grammaire n'aide pas les élèves à s'améliorer à long terme, plusieurs enseignants persistent à croire qu'ils doivent corriger toutes les fautes. Cet article rend compte de l'attitude d'élèves d'anglais comme langue étrangère lorsqu'on leur fait des commentaires positifs, motivants et accompagnés de suggestions sur des façons de s'améliorer. Plusieurs des élèves ont appris à accepter ce genre de rétroaction, mais beaucoup d'entre eux voulaient qu'on corrige également toutes les fautes grammaticales.

Introduction

A substantial amount of work has been published about giving feedback on foreign or second language written work (Fathman & Whalley, 1990; Ferris, 2002, 2003; Leki, 1991; Radecki & Swales, 1988; Robb, Ross, & Shortreed, 1986; Semke, 1984), and it has been suggested by many that teachers should avoid overcorrecting their students' writing (Hendrickson, 1980; Raimes, 1983; Semke, 1984; Zamel, 1985). Some even suggest that no grammatical errors should be marked (Truscott, 1996, makes the strongest argument).

However, many researchers and teachers believe that grammatical correction of some kind is necessary when responding to student writing. A number of researchers have noted that teachers even feel obligated to correct grammatical errors in their learners' written work. For example, Dohrer (1991) points out that many teachers (and even students) consider the number of marked errors to be a justification for the grade given. Similarly, Keh (1990) notes that "red marks on students' papers may also 'prove' the teacher's superiority over students and demonstrate that the teacher is 'doing his/her job'" (p. 294). Ancker (2000) describes interviews with teachers from around the world who have expressed the same sentiment. This prevalent attitude results in the extensive marking of errors in student writing. And even as teachers feel the need to mark errors, students also want correction (Leki, 1991).

However, what about the research that says that grammatical correction is not the best way to respond to students' writing? Teachers continue to mark grammatical errors although "the literature abounds with proof of the futility of marking errors in both native and non-native student writing" (Leki, 1991, p. 204). If teachers decide that they want to try alternative ways of commenting on students' writing, how can they justify the change to themselves and to their students? With this question in mind, the current study is a report of one attempt to change the attitudes of three groups of EFL students toward their teacher's feedback on written work. This was conducted through a series of chats in class, an emphasis on nongrammatical feedback on written exercises, and self-evaluation surveys.

Attitudes and Effectiveness of Feedback

Every language teacher knows the desire to mark all a student's errors. We spend hours marking students' papers with circles, underlining errors, and using various editing symbols, only to see the same errors appear on the following assignment. Why is this? What happens to all the time we spend on marking all those errors? Is it wasted time?

According to several researchers, yes, we have wasted our time marking students' grammatical errors. Ferris (1995) points out that "despite the perceived importance of the role of the teacher in responding to student writing, research in both L1 and L2 student writing provides very little evidence that such feedback actually helps the students' writing improve" (p. 34). But the desire to continue marking student errors is strong. For example, even reporting the apparent futility of error correction, Ferris claims that students do benefit from grammar comments and suggestions about organization and content. And Leki (1990), for example, points out that students want every error marked, although she also points out that many students simply look at their grade and not the teacher's corrections and comments.

So although students want to see their work corrected, a substantial amount of evidence has been presented that calls the effectiveness of this practice into question. For example, Robb et al. (1986) conducted a study of various types of feedback with four groups: correction group (teacher corrected all errors but did not comment on content or organization); coded feedback group (errors were marked with a code); uncoded feedback group (errors were marked with a highlighter); and marginal feedback group (the number of errors per line was indicated, but no errors were identified). They found that none of the feedback types resulted in long-term grammatical improvement and concluded that their results did not support the practice of marking grammatical errors extensively. They suggest that teachers use their time to respond to "more important aspects of student writing" (p. 91). As Raimes (1983) explains, "understanding and producing accurate grammatical forms is a parallel activity to composing" (p. 267), but it should not become the central focus of a teacher's feedback. Thus teachers' efforts should be expended on responding to content and composition-based issues rather than correcting grammatical errors. Mechanical errors can be dealt with in a number of alternative manners, from error logs to focused mini-lessons (Ferris, 2002).

It is important also to mention that the research does show that making comments about content and organization does help students to improve the quality of their writing. Hedgecock and Lefkowitz (1996) cite other authors (Sheppard, 1992; Kepner, 1991) who have come to the same conclusion: form-focused feedback is not as effective as content feedback in terms of eventual attainment.

Additional evidence can be found in Kepner (1991), who in a comparative study of feedback types (content feedback vs. grammatical correction) found that students who received only content feedback produced writing that had more "higher-level propositions" (better content) than students who received grammar-only feedback. In addition, students who received surface-level feedback did not produce fewer errors than the uncorrected group. In addition, Hillocks (1986) and Truscott (1996) both reviewed many research studies and concluded that in most of them, teachers' comments on grammar were shown to have little or no long-term effect on students' writing.

Even those who support the use of grammatical correction of writing assignments show results that can be interpreted as illustrating the ineffectiveness of this type of correction. For example, Fathman and Whalley (1990), in a comparative study of four groups of students (no feedback, grammar feedback only, content feedback only, content and grammar feedback), found that grammatical correction was helpful from the first draft to the revision stage of a single assignment, but provided no evidence that suggested long-term grammatical improvement. Interestingly, even the group that received no comments at all made short-term improvements in both grammatical accuracy and content.

Semke (1984) found that German-as-a-foreign-language students who received comments on content wrote much more than students who received grammatical corrections. Similarly, Gee (1972) studied native English-speaking students in three groups who received praise, no comments, or criticism (on superficial mechanical/grammatical errors and on content and style) and found that both the negative criticism and no-comments groups wrote less than the group that received praise.

Additional support for this approach comes from Dragga (1985, 1988), who recommends "praiseworthy grading" as a strategy to focus students' attention on what works well in their writing as opposed to what they do wrong. Many teachers and students in his study concluded that this positive emphasis on feedback was "ultimately rewarding" (1988, p. 47).

All this research leads to a dilemma for teachers. Radecki and Swales (1988) explain that if teachers "do not surface-correct but respond to a writer's meaning, their credibility among their students can be impaired" (p. 364). As mentioned above, most students expect correction, and many teachers feel the need to justify their grading and superiority. But for those noting the tendency of research to downplay the usefulness of this grammatical correction with respect to long-term improvement, something needs to be done to help justify a change. Radecki and Swales say that "teachers must intervene and change student attitudes; one way for teachers to change their students is by sharing with them the research in writing. Thus they could possibly vindicate their methods and reputation" (p. 364). This might be an effective way for teachers to address the problem. By teaching their students about the research findings, they may be able to help them accept a different approach to feedback. Similarly, Schulz (1996, 2001) suggests that teachers and students talk and explore varying points of view in order to avoid conflicts and to maximize positive attitudes toward the teacher's chosen path of instruction.

If we accept the accuracy of the research indicating limited-effectiveness error correction of student writing, we will see a need to negotiate an understanding between teachers and students about feedback techniques, especially as Radecki and Swales (1988) describe. Considering this, the approach taken in the current study was to see if it would be possible for high-intermediate EFL university students to accept the change from an emphasis on grammatical correction to feedback mostly on content and rhetorical issues in their writing assignments.

Changing Students' Attitudes

A major factor in my decision to try to move away from a reliance on grammar-focused feedback on writing assignments came from sources that discussed the possibility of changing students' attitudes toward classroom practices. Mantle-Bromley (1995) explains the nature of attitude theory involving three components: attitude, cognition, and behavior. In order to promote attitudinal change, one proposed suggestion is to have a classroom environment that is "one of 'change and novelty'" (p. 374). As a result, students are forced to consider their attitudes, and the potential for change is created.

An example comes from Winer (1992), who reports on the attitudes of student teachers toward writing and the teaching of writing. Most of her 100 graduate student participants started a training course with a negative attitude toward writing in general. Winer explains that her students' complaints came from their own experiences as students of writing, when there was "an undue emphasis on superficial errors in grammar and spelling without regard to content ... and a nonsupportive, nonsympathetic attitude on the part of the teacher" (p. 61). After starting her course with an attitude survey, Winer created a series of activities based on journal-writing, peer feedback, and teacher-student conversations that were used to help these student teachers change their attitudes about writing. They were asked to do the same writing assignments they were giving their students so that they could measure how interesting or boring each was. They were also asked to revise their own work so that they could understand how their students would feel when forced to revise. And they were specifically coached on how to give feedback in a positive way that would encourage their students, not crush them under the burden of being "punished" by rewriting. Winer reports that by the end of the one-semester course, most student teachers in her class did indeed change their attitudes toward writing and teaching writing by being forced to look at the issues in a novel way.

With all this in mind, the following study was developed to answer this question: Can EFL university students accept an emphasis on comments about content and suggestions for improving the quality of their writing instead of a focus on grammatical corrections?

Method

Participants

The participants for this study were three groups of high-intermediate students enrolled in a sixth-semester English-language course in a large public university in Colombia. All the students spoke Spanish as their native language and were modern language majors studying both English and French as foreign languages in order to graduate as licensed teachers. The first five semesters of language study in English were focused on general skill-building, and the sixth semester was dedicated to putting the basic skills into practice through extensive writing.

The observations for this study were made with three groups of students. The first group was from 1997 (14 students), the second from 1999 (16 students), and the third from 2000 (24 students). The basic material covered in each group was the same (writing development from paragraphs to essays, various genres of essays, and research writing), with changes in the presentation of material reflecting the instructor's own development in the theory and practice of nontraditional teaching and evaluation, with a focus on multiple intelligence theory and on teaching for understanding.

Ethnographic Methods

Presentation of new ideas. In addition to the regular topics of the course, which were covered over an 18-week semester, a small amount of class time was spent on explaining various perspectives on marking students' essays. The first such chat took place in the second week of the semester before any written assignments had been graded and had as its primary objective to introduce research about the effectiveness of grammatical correction in improving written language. The teacher asked the students questions and listened to them, making notes about their responses in her journal. A separate journal was kept for each course.

The first question the teacher asked during the first chat was, "How have your previous language teachers responded to your written assignments?" This question was designed to elicit responses from the students in each group and to start them thinking about what they had experienced in the past. After having a chance to respond, the students were asked, "What would you *like* your teachers to do?" The purpose of this question was to introduce the affective dimension of feedback to see if what students had received was what they really wanted at an emotional level.

After these questions and responses, the instructor explained that she was going to describe some research on the topic of providing grammatical corrections for composition assignments. The first article presented was Semke (1984). The instructor began by describing the four experimental groups, writing each on the board (1. comments only, 2. corrections only, 3. corrections with comments, and 4. student self-correction). Then she asked the students, "Can you predict which group improved the most after one semester of work?" When the students had had the opportunity to give their opinion (the number of votes was written next to each experimental group), the instructor explained Semke's findings. The group that improved the least was group 4: student self-correction. The group that improved the most both in terms of accuracy and fluency was group 1: comments only. The students who received grammatical correction either by itself or combined with comments on content did improve, but not as much as the first group.

This same format was used for introducing additional research by Cardelle and Corno (1981). They had four research groups: 1. praise, 2. criticism (grammatical correction), 3. criticism plus praise, and 4. no feedback. Of the four groups, the combined group (group 3) made the most improvement over the time of the study, and also students were more motivated by that type of combined feedback. After reviewing the results of these studies, the last question in this chat was, "How would you like me to respond to your written assignments?"

The students continued the semester writing a great deal in both their journals and in other assignments and essays. The assignments in the first six weeks of the semester were focused on developing paragraph structure in

English, and the feedback on these early assignments consisted mostly of positive comments about the development of ideas with specific suggestions for improving content, organization, or rhetoric. In general, little attention was given to grammatical errors.

The first self-evaluation took place during the seventh week of the semester (see Appendix), followed by the second chat in the eighth week. After receiving the teacher's mid-term evaluation of their work, the students were asked these questions: "What is your opinion of the way I am responding to your writing?" and "What do you remember about the research I mentioned at the beginning of the semester?"

The third chat occurred in the 10th week of classes after the teacher had returned an essay assignment that had received only grammatical corrections as a contrast to the other feedback that she had been giving. The first question was, "How do you feel right now after receiving the essay with grammatical corrections?" Then the students were asked to reflect on the feelings they had on other days when the teacher had returned assignments with comments on the content and organization and little focus on grammar. They were then asked, "Do you feel different with these two types of correction?"

The second self-evaluation was collected in the 12th week of classes (see Appendix), followed by the fourth chat. The students were asked the following question: "After receiving mostly comments on content, how do you feel about your writing?" After listening to their responses, the teacher explained that even many native speakers make grammatical and spelling errors when writing. Because of this, the goal for these EFL students should not be to slow the development of their ideas by examining surface-level errors. Instead, it should be to help them reach a level where they could clearly express their ideas despite a few remaining errors. The teacher explained again that the comments on content had been provided with that specific goal in mind: to give the students the tools needed to be confident to write a text that made sense and that communicated a clear idea. The final self-evaluation was given during the 14th week of class (see Appendix).

Comments on essays and journals. The primary origin of the writing on which feedback was provided was a journal that each student kept and that contained all in-class work. Additional feedback was given on periodic formal paragraph and essay assignments (approximately one per month). The teacher-researcher collected the journals every two to three weeks, read the various assignments, and made comments, mostly on the content of what was written, but with occasional grammatical corrections or suggestions when the problems were consistent or serious. Most grammatical errors were overlooked in favor of a focus on encouragement so that the students would write more and increase their fluency. The comments on the first drafts of the essays focused on improving organization, coherence, and the presentation of ideas (justification, details, etc.). The final drafts generally received comments about how well the students had acted on the comments on earlier drafts.

Self-Evaluations.

Students in the study were given three self-evaluations throughout each course in order to measure their attitudes. The first was conducted during the seventh week of class just before the teacher gave the students their mid-term evaluations of development in various areas. The second was administered in the 12th week of class. The last was done during the 16th week just before the end of the course. The self-evaluations looked for information about various aspects of the class and the students' own learning (see Appendix). In addition to questions about receiving feedback on their writing, these evaluations included questions about the students' goals for the course, their activities in English outside the class, and their desire for activities in class. At least one of the questions on each evaluation dealt with the students' opinions of the comments and corrections that were given on their written assignments.

Results and Discussion

Presentation of New Ideas

In the first chat, students were asked, "How have your previous language teachers responded to your written assignments?" The answers from all three groups revealed that teachers in the first five levels of English at the university generally had focused their energy on correcting grammatical errors on all written assignments. Little time was devoted to commenting on how to improve students' writing in ways other than grammatical correctness. When asked "What would you like your teachers to do?" most students explained that they felt that what they had been receiving was an appropriate way to deal with their errors (they mentioned that all their language teachers in both high school and university had the same style for responding to written work). They expected such correction, and as a result, accepted it. The students did note, however, that this type of feedback was not "nice," nor did it motivate them to write more or to be more creative in their efforts to complete assignments.

When the students were asked to predict which of the groups made the most progress in the Semke (1984) study, the majority in all three groups chose group 3, those who received both comments and corrections, followed by a number of students who chose group 2, correction only. They expressed surprise that the group that received comments only made the most improvement. The outcome of Cardelle and Corno's study was more in line with what the students expected. After seeing these results, their response to the final question—"How would you like me to respond to your written assignments?"—most students suggested a combination of comments on content along with grammatical corrections, although some expressed a preference for the status quo: primarily correcting errors.

It is interesting to note that the teacher's reputation of having an alternative manner of giving feedback became well known over the period covered by this study. The first group of students (1997) was initially the most reluctant to accept any type of feedback that was different from what they had previously known. By the second group (1999), the students were prepared for a change from the mold, but they still had to be convinced of the benefits of this new system of feedback. However, by the time the third group (2000) was taking the class, the word was out, and the students were expecting something else. The number of students enrolled in the course had also risen, specifically because the third group of students wished to experience this type of writing course. This made it easier to address the feedback issues with this group.

The second chat elicited responses similar to those in the first. Students were feeling more motivated about writing, but they still felt that more emphasis on grammar would help them continue to improve. When asked about the research cited at the beginning of the semester (specifically Semke's (1984) research), the students in the first two groups (1997 and 1999) were generally unable to remember the specific details. As a result, the researcher reviewed the studies again, and the students expressed their renewed understanding that comments on content could indeed work to improve motivation toward writing as well as fluency when faced with most assignments. By contrast, the 2000 group remembered more of the details from the research than the previous groups. This may have been because of their more accepting attitude toward a change in feedback methodology.

In the third chat, when asked how they felt after receiving an assignment with all the grammatical errors marked, most students responded negatively, especially those from the 2000 group. They said that they did not like to see their papers covered in red marks. When asked to compare this feeling with their attitude when they received comments on content, most responded that they felt more motivated than when the teacher simply marked grammar. However, several students pointed out that a balance between grammatical corrections and comments on content would be the best way for them to improve as writers.

In the fourth chat, when asked how they felt in general about the effects of feedback, most said that they had positive attitudes toward writing, something they admitted they did not have when beginning the semester. Many noted that they felt more confident as writers and that they enjoyed the writing tasks more than in previous courses. Most students, however, still pointed out that they felt that a number of the errors that they had made when writing had not been addressed much during the semester. After the teacher explained that the goal had been to get them to develop as writers who would be able to deal with a variety of writing assignments in English, almost all the students reported that they did in fact feel more confident when presented with a writing task. They explained that they thought this was due in part to the motivating comments they had received during the semester.

Comments on Essays and Journals

Students completed periodic formal essay assignments as well as daily journal activities. Typical comments from the teacher on formal essay drafts were:

> (On a penultimate draft) Clear objectives, nice organization and presentation of information. Good use of quotations to explain and support your ideas. You met the first two objectives that you set out for yourself, but you only briefly discuss the third (about education). You should review the objectives in the conclusion to remind the reader (and yourself) that you have met them. (1997)

> (On a final draft) Good work. I'm impressed with the changes you have made. Good use of quotation to support your opinion. Good reference list—complete and accurate. Better grammatical control (there are some errors that remain, but nothing serious). (1997)

> (On a final draft) You have made some good changes since the first draft. You have explained how Magroll and hopelessness are the main points of your essay—it is much more clear now. You have also added citations that explain where the ideas come from, which is good. (1999)

In the formal essay feedback, the focus for early drafts was on making global improvements in the organization and presentation of ideas. Comments on final drafts mentioned how the students had progressed as well as areas that could be improved. In contrast, the following are examples of the teacher's comments on journal entries.

> Wow! What a story! You and your partner have a wild imagination! I guess I should say "congratulations"!? I was truly surprised by the ending. (1999)

> You have a very well-done, organized and colorful journal. You have a lot of ideas and you write about everything; that's great! Like when you wrote about dreams. I used to have dreams almost every night. I wish I could remember everything. (2000)

> First of all, I want to comment on your three favorites. Yes, your headline poem is very nice, as your classmates' comments reflect. And

I'm glad that you liked it. That is very important when you are developing your writing. If you aren't pleased with your work, there is a tendency to stop writing. And I hope you are pleased with other things you have written—I would like to see you continue improving! (2000)

The primary purpose of the comments on journal entries was to motivate the students and to highlight their communication of ideas. With this in mind, the teacher tried to choose specific pieces and respond to them at a personal or emotional level. According to research by Dragga (1985, 1988) and others, this type of response to the communicated message motivates the student to continue to write.

Self-Evaluations

In the first self-evaluation, of 24 students in the 2000 group, 22 responded to the question: "Which type of feedback do you think is more effective to help you improve your written English: a: comments on content or b: grammatical corrections." From the 1999 group, all 16 students responded to this question, whereas in the 1997 group, 13 of the 14 students responded.

Despite emphasis in the class away from grammatical corrections and toward the implications of the research, which showed that marking grammar errors is of limited use, the most common attitude expressed by students from all three groups was a wish both for comments on content and for corrections of grammar. Many students explained that content-based comments made them feel good because they could see that their message was being received by a responsive reader, and as a result they were motivated to write more. However, they also noted that in order to recognize mistakes and make corrections, they needed more grammatical correction. Some students were not able to appreciate the importance of comments on rhetorical and organizational problems in their writing.

In the group from 2000, 16 of the 22 students answering this question suggested that both comments and corrections were important for improved writing. In 1999, 12 of 16 students agreed with this point of view, and in 1997, 12 out of 13 were in agreement.

The following comments illustrate this viewpoint.

I think both can help us to improve our writing because it is a combination that involves the academic and affective part of everyone. (2000)

I think both are most important because it's good to see what other people think about a subject or topic. It can be useful for you as a person and as a writer. On the other hand, I think that someone who can show you what your errors are is giving to you an opportunity to learn or correct something. (2000)

JoELLEN M. SIMPSON

The comments on content let me know if my writing is easy to understand, give me more confidence and furthermore it is nice to listen opinions; and it is also important the corrections in grammar because that way I know my mistakes and I can learn from them. (1999)

Sometimes I feel good when I don't see correction about my grammar, but sometimes it is necessary. (1999)

These examples demonstrate a certain degree acceptance that comments on content can be useful. These students express the positive affective results of this type of Dragga-style "praiseworthy" grading, but at the same time they note that grammar correction still plays an important role for them in their development as writers in a foreign language, just as Cardelle and Corno (1981) found.

The following set of comments helps illustrate the range of varying students' attitudes to comments on content; these other individuals seem to be much more willing than those above to accept that for long-term improvement, comments on the content and organization of writing can be more beneficial than specific grammatical corrections.

Grammar isn't sufficient to write well. We always write about something or someone, for example: I can use well the grammar, but in the writing my ideas can be contradictories or don't have them sense. (1999)

Grammar is important, but the most important is content correction because with content correction we can know about the structure of an English paragraph. (1997)

I feel grammar correction is important, but not too much. So is more important content correction because grammar will improve with the practice. (1997)

This final example clearly reflects what several researchers insist on: grammatical accuracy improves with practice (Truscott, 1996; Semke, 1984; among others), rather than with extensive correction of errors. However, because of the time-consuming nature of marking every grammatical error, many teachers decide to reduce the amount of writing that their students do (Kepner, 1991). This reduces the time they need to respond, but at the same time diminishes the number of opportunities the students have for improvement through practice. Writing does not have to be a punishment for the students and the teacher; it can be much more communicative. If a teacher uses a communicative style of responding, the teacher and students alike can learn to see writing as an enjoyable medium for language practice.

Although most of the students changed their attitudes and came to accept that comments on content were valuable, one from the 2000 group specifically pointed out that although comments on content expressed the teacher's opinions, this was not perceived as helpful.

> Corrections on grammar improve my writing because correction on content only give me opinion of my journal but no more. (2000)

This judgment appears to be reflected in research by Burkland and Grimm (1986), who found that students preferred criticism (in other words, grammatical correction) "and had an ambivalence about praise" (p. 242). Leki (1990) also noted that many students do not consider praise to be useful. The status quo in favor of grammatical correction is strong, and it appears that in any group there will be a few students who refuse to accept a change.

Thus it is notable that every year, a small group of student opinions did in fact reflect a preference for grammatical correction. Five students of 22 in the 2000 group expressed their preference for this type of feedback, and four of 16 from 1999 had the same opinion. And one student out of 13 from the 1997 group suggested that grammar was more important than content. These excerpts illustrate students' attitudes in this connection.

> I think the most effective to help me to improve my writing is correction on grammar because if you make the respective corrections I will see my faults. (2000)

> I need to improve my grammar to make good contents. (1999)

This group of students was unable to accept the change in perspective on the feedback to their writing. However, most did come to accept comments on content as an important element in feedback.

With regard to the question "Did you study the grammatical corrections that I made in order to try to learn from your errors? Why or why not?"—in the second round of self-evaluations—almost all the students said that they did indeed study the corrected errors. Many students wrote comments like this:

> Yes because I really want to learn from my errors and don't do them each time I want to write about the same idea. (1997)

> Yes because I would have to find my mistakes and I will like to learn about grammar. (1997)

> Yes, I did because with the grammatical correction I can improve my others works. And I try to improve more. (1999)

> Yes, I did, however it's difficult because we have mistakes that nobody have made us a correction so we were using that for a long time. (2000)

However, when returning work that had grammar corrections, the teacher herself noticed that few students seemed to take time in class to review the corrections or to ask questions about what was incorrect. Most of them read the end comment and the grade and put their papers away. This does not mean that the students did not later study the corrections, but there is always a question as to whether they learned from this type of correction. Other students in their self-evaluations were perhaps more honest about what they did with the teacher's corrections.

Not all of them because I forgot some of them. (1999)

Not really, sometimes this is not an excuse, but sometimes I feel really tired because of my work and I don't do my best in class. (2000)

I try to take that corrections into account, but unfortunately, I can't remember all of them when I'm writing. (2000)

Finally, on the final self-evaluation in response to the question "Do you feel that you write with fewer mistakes now than at the beginning of the course? Why?" the students reported positive results.

I feel I have improved.

I think I am more careful when I am writing.

I feel happy because I noted that I have improved my English.

Yes, I feel that each mistake goes away while I am writing.

This suggests that despite the change in emphasis away from the kind of grammatical correction that so many students appeared to prefer at the outset, or maybe because of it, students ended the course feeling much more positive about their ability to write. They had more confidence and worried less about superficial errors.

Conclusions

Some research suggests that it is a waste of time for teachers meticulously to mark every error students make in their written work. Despite this body of research, teachers and students continue to believe that corrections are necessary. If a teacher decides to accept a low-grammatical-correction stance in giving feedback in favor of an emphasis on content-based feedback, he or she needs to know if this will be accepted by the students and even by colleagues. In answer to the research question "Can EFL university students accept an emphasis on comments about content and suggestions for improving the quality of the writing instead and emphasis on corrections on grammar?" this report provides some evidence that it is indeed possible to modify students' opinions about feedback.

During three one-semester writing courses, three groups of students were exposed to an alternative approach to feedback through a series of short chats describing the relevant research and through the personal experience of receiving mostly motivating, positive feedback with suggestions for improvement. Based on this exposure, students' attitudes began to change. Although not everyone grew to accept the kind of praiseworthy grading recommended by Dragga (1985, 1988), most did learn to accept content feedback as an important part of learning how to write in a foreign language.

This study is not a rigorous experimental study with control and experimental groups, but as an ethnographic-type study, the comments expressed can be taken to represent the attitudes of these particular students under the specific circumstances described. For many EFL teachers in similar situations, this may provide the motivation to move away from relying exclusively on extensive grammar corrections toward a feedback style that is more concerned with content, organization, and other communicative issues. The research suggests that this is likely to be beneficial and effective for our students because they will be motivated to write based on the communication that is established with the teacher and others, and also because the teacher can assign more work if the grading-marking time is reduced. This results in more practice for the students, which can provide them with opportunities for continued improvement. The problem for individual teachers is to change our paradigm in order to accept this different approach to feedback and at the same time to help the students understand it and accept it; this long-term research project has provided evidence that such a change in attitude is possible.

The Author

JoEllen M. Simpson, after having been a full professor in the Universidad del Valle in Cali, Colombia, is now the General Director of the Centro Cultural Colombo Americano, the binational center in Cali. Her research interests are in the areas of feedback and contrastive rhetoric.

References

Ancker, W. (2000). Errors and corrective feedback: Updated theory and classroom practice. *English Language Teaching Forum, 38*(4), 20-25.

Burkland, J., & Grimm, N. (1986). Motivating through responding. *Journal of Teaching Writing, 5*, 237-247.

Cardelle, M., & Corno, L. (1981). Effects on second language learning of variations in written feedback on homework assignments. *TESOL Quarterly, 15*, 251-261.

Dohrer, G. (1991). Do teachers' comments on students papers help? *College Teaching, 39*(2), 48-54.

Dragga, S. (1985). Praiseworthy grading. *Journal of Teaching Writing, 4*, 264-268.

Dragga, S. (1988). The effects of praiseworthy grading on students and teachers. *Journal of Teaching Writing, 7*, 41-50.

Fathman, A.K., & Whalley, E. (1990). Teacher response to student writing: Focus on form versus content. In B. Kroll (Ed.), *Second language writing: Research insights for the classroom* (pp. 178-190). Cambridge, UK: Cambridge University Press.

Ferris, D.R. (1995). Student reactions to teacher response in multiple-draft composition classrooms. *TESOL Quarterly, 29*, 33-53.

Ferris, D.R. (2002). *Treatment of error in second language student writing*. Ann Arbor, MI: University of Michigan Press.

Ferris, D.R. (2003). *Response to student writing: Implications for second language students*. Mahwah, NJ: Erlbaum.

Gee, T. (1972). Students' responses to teacher comments. *Research in the Teaching of English, 6*(2), 212-221.

Hedgcock, J., & Lefkowitz, N. (1996). Some input on input: Two analyses of student response to expert feedback in L2 writing. *Modern Language Journal, 80*, 287-308.

Hendrickson, J.M. (1980). The treatment of error in written work. *Modern Language Journal, 64*, 216-221.

Hillocks, G., Jr. (1986). The interaction of instruction, teacher comments, and revision in teaching the composing process. *Research in the Teaching of English, 16*, 261-278.

Keh, C.L. (1990). Feedback in the writing process: A model and methods for implementation. *ELT Journal, 44*, 294-304.

Kepner, C.G. (1991). An experiment in the relationship of types of written feedback to the development of second-language writing skills. *Modern Language Journal, 75*, 305-313.

Leki, I. (1990). Coaching from the margins: Issues in written response. In B. Kroll (Ed.), *Second language writing: Research insights for the classroom* (pp. 57-68). Cambridge, UK: Cambridge University Press.

Leki, I. (1991). The preferences of ESL students for error correction in college-level writing classes. *Foreign Language Annals, 24*, 203-218.

Mantle-Bromley, C. (1995). Positive attitudes and realistic beliefs: Links to proficiency. *Modern Language Journal, 79*, 372-386.

Radecki, P.M., & Swales, J.M. (1988). ESL student reaction to written comments on their written work. *System, 16*(3), 355-365.

Raimes, A. (1983). Anguish as a second language: Remedies for composition teachers. In A. Freedman, I. Pringle, & J. Yalden (Eds.), *Learning to write: First language/second language* (pp. 258-272). London: Longman.

Robb, T., Ross, S., & Shortreed, I. (1986). Salience of feedback on error and its effect on EFL writing quality. *TESOL Quarterly, 20*, 83-93.

Schulz, R.A. (1996). Focus on form in the foreign language classroom: Students' and teachers' views on error correction. *Foreign Language Annals, 29*, 343-364.

Schulz, R.A. (2001). Cultural differences in student and teacher perceptions concerning the role of grammar instruction and corrective feedback: USA-Colombia. *Modern Language Journal, 85*, 244-258.

Semke, H.D. (1984). The effects of the red pen. *Foreign Language Annals, 17*, 195-202.

Sheppard, K. (1992). Two feedback types: Do they make a difference? *RELC Journal, 23*, 102-110.

Truscott, J. (1996). Review article: The case against grammar correction in L2 writing classes. *Language Learning, 46*, 327-369.

Winer, L. (1992). Spinach to chocolate: Changing awareness and attitudes in ESL writing teachers. *TESOL Quarterly, 26*, 57-79.

Zamel, V. (1985). Responding to student writing. *TESOL Quarterly, 19*, 79-101.

Appendix

First Self-Evaluation

1. What has been one thing that you have learned so far?
2. What skill do you feel you need the most work in (reading, writing, speaking, listening)?

3. What could you do to improve this? Will you do it? Why or why not?
4. What can I do to help you improve this skill?
5. Which type of feedback is more effective to help you improve your written English: a: comments on content or b: corrections of grammar? Why?
6. What would you like to see more of in the class?
7. What would you like to see eliminated from the class?

Second Self-Evaluation

1. What skill do you feel you have improved the most in so far in this course (reading, writing, speaking, listening)?
2. Did you study the grammatical corrections that I made in order to try to learn from your errors? Why or why not?
3. Have you done research writing before? If so, what is it? If not, what do you think it will be?
4. What would you like to see more of in the second half of the course?

Third Self-Evaluation

1. In this course, what has been the most important thing you learned?
2. What skill do you feel you have improved the most in this semester (speaking, listening, reading, writing)?
3. What skill do you feel you need the most work in?
4. During this semester, what did you do outside of class to improve your English language skills?
5. Regarding research writing, what do you think you still need to learn?
6. Do you feel that you write with fewer mistakes now than at the beginning of the course? Why?
7. Why are you majoring in Modern Languages (what are your goals)?
8. Do you think you have done everything you can in this class to help you meet your goals? Why or why not?

University Students' Beliefs and Attitudes Regarding Foreign Language Learning in France

Nathalie Piquemal and Robert Renaud

This study is based on a survey of 1,305 university students enrolled in English and other foreign-language classes across year levels in four major universities in France. It explores the factors that promote or hinder multilingualism, with special attention to the following questions: What are the beliefs and attitudes of students enrolled in various postsecondary institutions across France toward learning a foreign language? How do these beliefs and attitudes change as students progress from beginning first-year students to upper years? The results suggest that the reasons first-year students typically have for studying a foreign language have more to do with internal factors (e.g., personal attitude) than with external factoars (e.g., social value). Moreover, this trend becomes more pronounced with upper-year students whose motivation to learn a foreign language compared with that of first-year students is influenced less by perceived societal beliefs and more by intrinsic reasons.

Ce projet de recherche repose sur un sondage auprès de 1 305 étudiants inscrits à des cours d'ALE ou d'autres langues étrangères de divers niveaux dans quatre grandes universités en France. Il porte sur les facteurs qui favorisent ou entravent le multilinguisme et cherche à répondre aux questions suivantes : Quelles croyances et attitudes les étudiants inscrits à diverses institutions universitaires en France entretiennent-ils face à l'apprentissage d'une langue étrangère? Dans quelle mesure ces croyances et attitudes changent-elles à mesure que les étudiants passent des cours de première année à des cours plus avancés? Les résultats indiquent que les raisons qui poussent les étudiants en première année à étudier une langue étrangère sont typiquement davantage liées à des facteurs internes (p. ex. attitude individuelle) qu'externes (p. ex. valeur sociale). De plus, cette tendance s'accentue chez les étudiants plus avancés, dont la motivation à apprendre une langue étrangère est encore moins influencée par des croyances sociales et plus par des raisons intrinsèques.

Introduction

Although the idea that the learner's beliefs about and attitudes toward foreign language learning are key in facilitating or hindering success is not new, little research explores these beliefs and attitudes in relation to broader social contexts of foreign language learning in varying institutions, and with a large sample of learners from various year levels. Indeed, with the exception of Rifkin's (2000) research in the United States, much of the research on foreign language learners' own personal beliefs has focused on beginning language classes from one institution, usually in the US, leaving out two important factors, namely, the perception of societal norms, also referred to as socio-suggestive norms (Miele, 1982) and the evolution of beliefs and attitudes across year levels. Furthermore, although the literature has addressed the need to link sociocultural factors with foreign language learning (Demmert, 1993; Miele; Pennycook, 1994; Strevens, 1978; Turner, 1974), much of the research to date has focused on case studies that highlight individual social circumstances in foreign language learning and mainly in classroom contexts (Graham & Brown, 1996; Martin, 1990; Norton & Toohey, 2001).

Therefore, the purpose of the research reported in this article is to gain a better understanding of the factors that promote or hinder multilingualism, with special attention to learners' beliefs and attitudes toward foreign language learning, namely, English, as well as the effect of contextual influences or socio-suggestive norms, on foreign language learning in France. By socio-suggestive norms, we mean perceived factors such as the social value of foreign language learning, pedagogical practice, public attitudes, opportunities for multilinguals, and government initiatives. This study set out to answer two questions. First, what are the beliefs and attitudes that students enrolled in postsecondary institutions across France have toward learning English as a foreign language? Second, how do these beliefs and attitudes change as students progress from first-year students to upper years? More specifically, students' beliefs and attitudes were assessed in terms of the effect of social norms on foreign language learning (i.e., how much students think society values foreign language learning), perceived advantages of foreign language learning, the role of instruction in foreign language learning, personal attitudes toward foreign language learning, and personal experiences in foreign language learning. Central to this study is the recognition that students' motivation is inherently shaped by their beliefs and attitudes toward learning a foreign language (Gardner, 1985; Gardner & Lambert, 1972).

This article reports the results of a survey of 1,305 university students enrolled in foreign language classes (English and at least one other foreign language) across three year levels in each of four universities located in varying geographical locations in France. The findings of this study support several implications that will help better inform teacher practice and policy development in France and in other countries where students exhibit similar beliefs and attitudes.

     NATHALIE PIQUEMAL and ROBERT RENAUD

Review of the Literature and Conceptual Framework

The idea that students' beliefs about and attitudes toward foreign language learning have an effect on their success or failure in achieving competence in a foreign language is well documented (Horwitz, 1988; Jernigan, 2001; Kern, 1995; Miele, 1982; Rifkin, 2000; Strevens, 1978). One focus of research exploring students' beliefs about and attitudes toward foreign language learning contends that individuals' positive or negative beliefs and perceptions about foreign language learning have a similarly positive or negative effect on their success. Mantle-Bromley (1995), for example, argues that positive beliefs about foreign language learning combined with a positive learning environment such as trust-building between teacher and student facilitate foreign language learning and that negative beliefs hinder success. Horwitz argues that students' beliefs about foreign language learning affect the learning strategies that these students choose and contends that teachers cannot afford to ignore their students' beliefs if they wish to implement teaching methods that are efficient and well received. Jernigan explored the role that students' beliefs about foreign language learning play in their decisions to continue or discontinue their studies and found that teachers plan discussions with their students around these beliefs. MacIntyre and Gardner (1994) argue that language anxiety related to issues of pronunciation has a negative effect on foreign language learning. Similarly, Horwitz (1991) argues that anxiety influences the communication strategies used by foreign language learners. In a different yet related way, Kamhi-Stein (2003) used four case studies and found that students' beliefs about both their heritage language (as valuable or not) and reading in English and in Spanish affected their reading behavior. This shows that students' beliefs about the social value of their heritage language are likely to affect student learning. Therefore, this article focuses on examining students' perceived social value of learning a foreign language such as English and the extent to which such perception is embedded in students' motivation.

More closely related to our research focus on external and internal motivation, Gardner's (1985) and Gardner and Lambert's (1972) socio-educational model of integrative/instrumental motivation provides valuable insights into the role that attitudes, motivation, and orientations play in second-language achievement. They identified two kinds of orientations: integrative orientation, which refers to a desire to learn a second language in order to identify with the language community; and instrumental orientation, which refers to practical reasons for learning a second language such as career or course credit. Their findings showed that second-language achievement was positively related to instrumental motivation and even more strongly related to integrative motivation (also see Masgoret & Gardner, 2003).

Our study identifies similar factors, including perceived opportunities, personal attitudes, and experiences toward foreign language learning while offering additional insights into the perceived social value of foreign language learning. This includes not only students' perceptions on foreign language learning as socially and culturally bound (Dörnyei, 2003) or students' desire to learn a foreign language because of a desire to be accepted by the new linguistic community (Gardner, 1985), but also,and perhaps more important, the extent to which students believe that the society in which they live values foreign language learning.

Sociolinguistic theories have been developed to explain the social nature of learning as it applies to learning a foreign language. Gumperz and Hymes (1972) stressed the role of cultural beliefs in learning to speak, which is essentially a reflection of the continual interplay between linguistic structure and its sociocultural context. In particular, Hymes' (1972) work on the notion of the ethnography of speaking stresses the importance of looking at the cultural organization of language use in order to understand shared speaking practices and shared conceptions about the role of language in any given culture. Therefore, fundamental to the sociolinguistic view that language is used in relation to a specific social and cultural context (Hymes) and that learning is shaped by sociocultural participation in a given community (Rogoff, 1994) is the assumption that many of the characteristics of foreign language learning are dependent not only on teaching methods and learning strategies, but also on sociocultural influences. This view is also echoed by Norton and Toohey (2001), who argue that approaches leading to a better understanding of what promotes foreign language learning should "focus not only on learners' internal characteristics, learning strategies, or linguistic outputs but also on the reception of their actions in particular sociocultural communities" (p. 308).

Another perspective that attempts to explain the effects of social-suggestive norms in foreign language learning is the influence of community and second-language teaching as developed by Ashworth (1985). Ashworth explored how varying communities (geopolitical (neighborhoods), common interests (family, speech community), and professional (educational institutions) affect learners' attitudes, expectations, and aspirations toward foreign language learning. In particular, Ashworth explained that socioeconomic status affects students' attitudes toward foreign language learning, which is key in determining who attends language classes and how well the students do. Ashworth suggests that teachers need to be responsive to inequities among foreign language learners by encouraging special programs and giving a more influential role to local neighborhoods. Moreover, Ashworth also explored how national policies (immigration, education, language rights, economic and employment policies) affect foreign language teaching and learning (what languages are prioritized, who will teach what language

NATHALIE PIQUEMAL and ROBERT RENAUD

to whom, how well the students will do). In sum, Ashworth suggests that in order to better benefit students, language teachers need to "develop a political awareness and sensitivity" (p. 103) to the philosophies that underlie national policies and to emerging socioeconomic trends in communities, with special attention to the unmet needs of individuals.

In keeping with Rifkin (2000), who contends that "in order to develop plans to overcome learners' counterproductive beliefs about foreign language learning, we must first understand exactly what those beliefs are" (pp. 394-395), our study recognizes a need to explore specific beliefs about foreign language learning in order to better inform pedagogical practices, government policies, and program development. If teachers and researchers are more cognizant of students' beliefs and attitudes toward foreign language learning, they might be in a better position to foster learning strategies that address (and challenge when necessary) these beliefs. Similarly, if policymakers are sensitized to the social, cultural, and historical factors that influence these beliefs, they might be in a better position to define educational goals by using these factors as a reference point for policy development.

As the global economy continues to develop, so too does the need for countries to prepare themselves such that they can better participate on an international level. One factor that seems to play a sizeable role in how well a country can continue to flourish in the 21st century is the ability of its population to learn the language(s) necessary for efficient communication with other nations. Recently, France has begun to recognize the need to promote multilingualism in the context of globalization. Previous French Minister of Education Jack Lang (2001) acknowledged that France cannot participate in the new economy through the medium of English or French only: "Tout montre que l'avenir de notre pays et des jeunes Européens impose la maîtrise d'au moins deux langues vivantes étrangères en plus de la langue maternelle" (p. 10), which translates as "Everything shows that the future of our country and of European Youth requires mastering at least two foreign languages besides the heritage language" (authors' translation). In such a framework, France has attempted to introduce foreign language teaching in primary classrooms (mainly English), besides the current mandatory study of two foreign languages in both junior and senior high school (one of which is generally English). Such an initiative responds to the growing concern for international participation as well as to the growing recognition of English as an international language. This type of initiative challenges, although not necessarily successfully, French language ideology around the societal belief that French, as an "almost recognized international language" and as a "national unifier" against regional languages, needs to be preserved and defended against the dominance of English, as well as against France's minority regional languages (Kasuya, 2001). Therefore, when exploring the beliefs and attitudes of foreign language learners in France, one needs to keep in mind some of the societal complexities, a significant one of which being that although English undoubtedly has a privileged position among foreign languages in France, it nonetheless faces an undeniable degree of defensiveness from those who believe that the French language is to be vigorously defended against the perceived global dominance of English (Kasuya, 2001; Calvet, 1999; Hagège, 1996).

Method

Participants

The participants were 1,305 university students enrolled in English language classes, ranging from 15 to over 200 students and studying at least one other foreign language such as Spanish, Italian, German, Japanese, Arabic, or Russian from four geographical locations in France: Université Paris IV, Université de Provence à Aix-en-Provence, Université de Perpignan, and Université du Var à Toulon. These universities were chosen because they are all located in large urban centers to which the researcher was granted access, and each offers language programs at all university year levels and in two main areas of study. The year levels covered in this study include first year (n=649), second (DEUG) (n=343), and third (Licence) year (n=313, equivalent to undergraduate in North America). Areas of study included LLCE (Lettres, Langues, et Cultures Etrangères) and LEA (Langues Etrangères Appliquées). The former field of study focuses mainly on literature, civilization, and history, whereas the latter focuses on more marketable fields such as economics, business administration, and law. All students enrolled in English classes at all three year levels were surveyed during the second semester (January-June) 2003. The approximate rate of response was 40% for first- and second-year students and 50% for third-year students.

All the students surveyed had studied English and at least one other foreign language before arriving at the university. These students studied English as well as a second (and sometimes a third) foreign language for between five and seven years before entering their university program. Students in France are required to select a first foreign language at the beginning of their junior high school program and a second half-way through. Students continue studying these languages until the end of their high school program, with the option of selecting a third foreign language at the beginning of their high school program. Studying at least two foreign languages in both junior and high school is mandatory in France. There is no selection process for university entrance. The high school diploma (Baccalauréat) is all that is required to enter a university program. Although first-year university students are not beginners in foreign language learning, their levels of language

NATHALIE PIQUEMAL and ROBERT RENAUD

proficiency vary greatly; by contrast, they are beginners in the field in which they have chosen to specialize (in this case either LLCE or LEA).

Survey Instrument

The survey instrument was developed in two stages (the survey was constructed by two researchers involved in an international study that involved three countries: Canada, France, and Japan). The first stage consisted of adapting items from existing instruments such as the Belief Inventory developed by Horwitz (BALLI, 1988), and the Strategy Inventory for Language Learning (SILL, Oxford, 1990). Additional questions were developed from individual interviews and focus group discussions in both Canada and in France. The final version contains 69 selected-response and six open-ended questions pertaining directly to students' beliefs and attitudes, 10 questions on demographics, four questions about the student's experience in learning a foreign language, and a general question that allows for any further response. The selected-response questions, which were the focus of the analysis in this study, were intended to assess the following factors: perceived social norms in foreign language learning, perceived advantages of foreign language learning, the role of instruction and instructional strategies in foreign language learning, personal beliefs and attitudes toward foreign language learning, and personal experiences in foreign language learning. Each question was answered using a 6-point Likert scale (from 1=strongly disagree to 6=strongly disagree) along with the option to answer "I do not wish to answer" or "I have no opinion." The questions aim at exploring both beliefs and attitudes, two factors that may help us better understand where language educators and policymakers should direct their efforts in order to facilitate success foreign language learning. For example, the statement "I respect people who speak more than one language"reflects an attitude that suggests a favorable evaluation of bilingualism, whereas the statement "Knowing a foreign language makes it easier to learn other subjects (such as sciences, mathematics, social studies, geography)" reflects a belief that there is a relationship between learning a foreign language and learning other subjects.

Procedure

After obtaining permission from deans and department heads, the first author approached professors individually to inform them about the research and to obtain their permission to distribute the surveys to the students. As the surveys were distributed at the beginning of the class, students were assured that (a) their participation was completely optional, (b) their responses would be kept confidential, and (c) whether they chose to participate had no effect on their course grade. Students were asked to complete the survey outside class time and to return their completed surveys to either a designated mailbox or their professor.

Results

To determine what latent constructs and their respective indicator items would be used to compare the latent mean differences across year levels, all 69 items were subjected to a principal components analysis with Promax rotation. More specifically, the purpose of this exploratory analysis was to develop a more parsimonious model consisting of only those items that would best reflect their intended factors. For each year level, a consistent factor structure that reflected the five subscales in the Foreign Language Questionnaire was obtained. The three items that loaded most strongly on a particular factor in each year was retained for the analyses. Thus the initial version of the abbreviated scale consisted of three items in each of the same five subscales as in the original version, leaving a total of 15 items. Preliminary confirmatory factor analyses using AMOS (version 5) was used to establish a baseline model that was more replicable across each of the three year levels. This resulted in the removal of one item, leaving a total of 14. The retained items and the factors they represent are listed in the Appendix. The means and standard deviations for each observed variable in each year are

Table 1
Observed Means and Standard Deviations for Observed Variables in the Social-Suggestive Norms in the Foreign Language Learning Questionnaire

Item and description	Year 1 (n=649)	Year 2 (n=343)	Year 3 (n=313)
SV1 government policies	3.69 (1.41)	3.37 (1.42)	3.51 (1.41)
SV2 normal part of life	3.59 (1.36)	3.33 (1.37)	3.30 (1.33)
SV3 becoming more interested	4.27 (1.18)	3.93 (1.28)	4.25 (1.08)
PO1 more educational opportunities	4.71 (1.14)	4.63 (1.20)	4.58 (1.20)
PO2 job advertisements	5.05 (0.98)	5.07 (1.07)	5.05 (0.91)
PO3 necessary to get a good job	4.63 (1.23)	4.72 (1.30)	4.57 (1.23)
TC1 classes important - beginner	5.18 (0.92)	5.31 (0.86)	5.24 (0.92)
TC2 classes important - intermediate	5.13 (0.92)	5.25 (0.85)	5.17 (0.93)
TC3 classes important - advanced	4.78 (1.23)	5.02 (1.08)	4.98 (1.06)
PA1 interesting activity	5.46 (0.74)	5.61 (0.62)	5.62 (0.53)
PA2 learn language and culture	5.27 (0.81)	5.37 (0.81)	5.41 (0.63)
PA3 know the speakers better	4.81 (1.11)	5.05 (0.99)	4.97 (0.95)
PE1 talk to native speakers	4.52 (1.28)	4.48 (1.41)	4.64 (1.31)
PE2 read newspaper	3.66 (1.57)	3.86 (1.49)	4.22 (1.27)

Note. Standard deviations in parentheses; Full wording for each item is listed in the Appendix.

NATHALIE PIQUEMAL and ROBERT RENAUD

listed in Table 1. Inspection of skewness and kurtosis for each variable revealed no significant departure from normality.

In looking at the students' beliefs and attitudes in each year, a couple of findings are noteworthy. From the mean values listed in Table 1, it appears that first-year students felt that the degree to which society values learning a foreign language was modest at best. For example, first-year students were only mildly convinced of the existence of government policies to encourage the French to learn foreign languages ($M=3.69$, $SD=1.41$). Interestingly, students in second and third years perceived even less societal value attached to learning foreign languages. However, the large standard deviations of the students' responses on the social value items show quite a bit of variability, with some students perceiving strong societal influence, whereas others thought the opposite. In contrast to the generally perceived weaker influence of social values, first-year students appeared to be intrinsically motivated

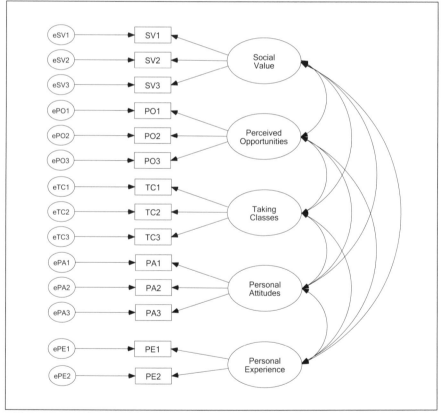

Figure 1. Baseline model depicting observed and latent variables representing beliefs and attitudes about foreign language learning.

Table 2
Baseline Model Standardized Parameter Estimates for Beliefs and
Attitudes About Foreign Language Learning (Year 1)

	SV	PO	TC	PA	PE	Error Variance
SV1 government policies	.44					1.60
SV2 normal part of life	.73					.87
SV3 becoming more interested	.42					1.13
PO1 more educational opportunities		.52				.95
PO2 job advertisements		.42				.80
PO3 necessary to get a good job		.64				.89
TC1 classes important—beginner			.71			.42
TC2 classes important—intermediate			.97	.05		
TC3 classes important—advanced			.57			1.08
PA1 interesting activity				.59		.35
PA2 learn language and culture				.57		.44
PA3 know the speakers better				.61		.77
PE1 talk to native speakers					.61	1.03
PE2 read newspaper					.49	1.86

Factor Correlations

	SV	PO	TC	PA	PE
SV	-				
PO	.17	-			
TC	.08	.29	-		
PA	−.01	.45	.41	-	
PE	.04	.28	.26	.60	-

Note. SV=Social value; PO=Perceived Opportunities; TC=Taking Classes; PA=Personal Attitudes; PE=Personal Experience;

toward learning a foreign language. Most first-year students tended to agree quite strongly that foreign language learning is an interesting activity (M=5.46, SD=0.74).

Before conducting the between-group comparisons of latent means, a single baseline model was tested with each group. A visual representation of the baseline model is shown in Figure 1, which depicts the five latent variables, their representative observed variables (i.e., survey items), and the error component associated with each observed variable. Byrne (2001) provides a relatively nontechnical introduction to the logic and representation of structural equation models. Somewhat analogous to the concept of variance accounted for in correlation or regression, two commonly used

Table 3
Baseline Model Standardized Parameter Estimates for Beliefs and Attitudes About Foreign Language Learning (Year 2)

	SV	PO	TC	PA	PE	Error Variance
SV1 government policies	.61					1.27
SV2 normal part of life	.73					.88
SV3 becoming more interested	.44					1.31
PO1 more educational opportunities		.48				1.11
PO2 job advertisements		.63				.68
PO3 necessary to get a good job		.72				.81
TC1 classes important - beginner			.68			.40
TC2 classes important - intermediate			.95			.07
TC3 classes important - advanced			.63			.70
PA1 interesting activity				.50		.29
PA2 learn language and culture				.67		.36
PA3 know the speakers better				.55		.68
PE1 talk to native speakers					.65	1.15
PE2 read newspaper					.59	1.43

Factor Correlations

SV	-				
PO	.26	-			
TC	−.17	.29	-		
PA	−.05	.45	.39	-	
PE	.04	.35	−.02	.52	-

Note. SV=Social value; PO=Perceived Opportunities; TC=Taking Classes; PA=Personal Attitudes; PE=Personal Experience;

indices that indicate the degree of similarity between the actual data covariances and those of the estimated values based on the parameters in the model are the comparative fit index (CFI) and the root mean square error of approximation (RMSEA), with values of 1.0 and 0.0 respectively indicating a perfect fit between the model estimates and the actual data. In general, a model that yields a CFI value close to .95 and a RMSEA close to .05 represents an acceptable fit (Hu & Bentler, 1999). The baseline model was found to fit the data fairly well in each group with Year 1 (CFI=.94, RMSEA=.04), Year 2 (CFI=.96, RMSEA=.04), and Year 3 (CFI=.91, RMSEA=.06). The baseline model standardized parameter estimates for Year 1, Year 2, and Year 3 are listed in Tables 2, 3, and 4 respectively. In each of the three year levels, the

Table 4
Baseline Model Standardized Parameter Estimates for Beliefs and
Attitudes About Foreign Language Learning (Year 3)

	SV	PO	TC	PA	PE	Error Variance
SV1 government policies	.34					1.76
SV2 normal part of life	.83					.56
SV3 becoming more interested	.43					.95
PO1 more educational opportunities		.49				1.09
PO2 job advertisements		.68				.44
PO3 necessary to get a good job		.71				.74
TC1 classes important - beginner			.72			.41
TC2 classes important - intermediate			.95			.09
TC3 classes important - advanced			.67			.62
PA1 interesting activity				.43		.23
PA2 learn language and culture				.45		.32
PA3 know the speakers better				.55		.63
PE1 talk to native speakers					.82	.55
PE2 read newspaper					.51	1.19

Factor Correlations

SV	-				
PO	.25	-			
TC	−.06	.15	-		
PA	.10	.08	.26	-	
PE	.11	.07	−.04	.46	-

Note. SV=Social value; PO=Perceived Opportunities; TC=Taking Classes; PA=Personal Attitudes; PE=Personal Experience;

error variances for some of the observed variables seem rather large (e.g., SV1, SV3, PE2) indicating that the amount of variance accounted for in each of these variables is relatively small compared with that of other observed variables such as TC2 and PA1. Although the variance accounted for by the observed variables could be improved by adding parameters to the baseline model, doing so would yield a more complex model that would not generalize across year levels as well as the current model.

Looking at Year 1 (Table 2), a few of the factors showed moderately strong correlations with one another. Personal Attitudes correlated with Perceived Opportunities, Taking Classes, and Personal Experience (.45, .41, and .60 respectively). This indicates that Year 1 students who are personally

Table 5
Latent Variable Means Across Year Levels

	SV	PO	TC	PA	PE
Year 2 (compared against Year 1)	−.21**	.02	.11*	.06	
	(.05)	(.05)	(.05)	(.04)	(.08)
Year 3 (compared against Year 2)	.06	−.06	−.06	.00	.24**
	(.05)	(.06)	(.06)	(.05)	(.09)
Year 3 (compared against Year 1)	−.11**	−.05	.05	.14**	.41**
	(.04)	(.05)	(.05)	(.03)	(.09)

Note. SV=Social value; PO=Perceived Opportunities; TC=Taking Classes; PA=Personal Attitudes; PE=Personal Experience; Standard Error in Parentheses; *p<.05; **p<.01.

interested in learning a foreign language are also likely to value both in- and out-of-class learning that will help them take better advantage of later career opportunities. This pattern was again found with Year 2, as Personal Attitudes correlated with Perceived Opportunities, Taking Classes, and Personal Experiences (.45, .39, and .52 respectively). In Year 3, however, the factors appeared to become more independent, with the strongest relationship between only Personal Attitudes and Personal Experience (.46).

The procedure used in AMOS to compare latent variable means between groups (i.e., year levels) requires that the means of one group be fixed to 0. Thus the values listed in Table 5 represent the differences between group means on each of the factors. Looking at the comparison between Year 1 and 2 with the mean values of Year 1 fixed to 0, Year 2 students seemed to be less convinced that society in general values learning a foreign language (SV= −.21). However, Year 2 students appeared to be more interested in learning a foreign language (PA=.16) and more appreciative of the value of taking classes (TC=.11). In comparing Year 2 and 3, Year 3 students reported having more personal experiences (PE=.24). These differences were confirmed further in the comparisons between Year 1 and 3. Compared with Year 1, the perception of society's value of learning a foreign language was lower among Year 3 students (SV=−.11). In addition, Year 3 students indicated that they had more personal interest (PA=.14) and personal experience (PE=.41) in learning a foreign language. In sum, the main finding that these results suggest is that many students appear to start learning a foreign language due more to internal reasons (e.g., personal interest) than external reasons (e.g., society thinks it is desirable or good). Looking at students in their second and third years of study, the influences of internal and external and reasons appear to be increasingly divergent, as upper-year students seem less concerned with how others might view studying a foreign language and more motivated by their own genuine interest.

Discussion

The purpose of this study was to determine the types of beliefs and attitudes of university students in France regarding their learning of a foreign language. As well, these beliefs and attitudes were compared across year levels. Overall, the results of this study suggest that the reasons first-year students typically give for studying a foreign language have more to do with internal factors (e.g., personal attitude) than with external factors (e.g., social value). Moreover, this trend becomes more pronounced with upper-year students whose motivation to learn a foreign language, compared with first-year students, is influenced less by perceived societal beliefs and more by intrinsic reasons.

First-year university students are generally recent high-school graduates, recipients of the national high school degree, le Baccalauréat, which in France symbolizes a socially valued rite of passage. This degree is considered a social *sine qua non* by French society, especially given the Ministry of Education's goal in 1985 to increase the number of high-school graduates to 80%. High-school students experience unquestionable pressure from friends, relatives, and the larger society to obtain this diploma. Once this degree is obtained, a significant pressure is off and new doors open. Students believe that this high-school degree will undoubtedly enable them to access postsecondary studies, particularly university studies. Indeed, in a recent article in a local newspaper, Beaud (2004, p. 18), a sociologist and researcher at the CNR (Centre National de Recherches Scientifiques), describes the Baccalauréat as a "passeport [qui] a toujours une fonction sociale fortement élevée … [un] examen qui donne aussi des droits sociaux comme l'accès à l'enseignement supérieur et le statut envié d'étudiant.… C'est un visa pour le monde universitaire," which translates as "passport [that] still has a significantly high social value … [an] exam that also provides social rights such as access to postsecondary education and to highly desired student status.… It is a visa for the university world" (authors' translation). At the end of high school, students may choose the area of study in which they wish to specialize. It is possible that armed with this degree, which carries important social value, first-year university students experience a great degree of enthusiasm largely due to external factors such as their own perceptions of how society values their degree and the pursuit of a postsecondary education. Given this general perception of how highly society values further education, it was interesting to find that this view was not as strong with respect to foreign language learning. In particular, first-year students thought that society viewed foreign language learning as only marginally important. Moreover, second- and third-year students judged the degree of societal value as lower than did their first-year cohorts. One possible explanation is that, as stated at the beginning of this article, France's collective consciousness appears to be somewhat conflicted when taking a stance on the importance of foreign languages. Indeed, although English is given a privileged position among foreign languages by the public, it tends to be simultaneously perceived as a threat to the French language given its increasing global dominance (Kasuya, 2001; Calvet, 1999; Hagège, 1996). Therefore, our young respondents may feel that the social value of foreign language learning is only marginally important because many French people may not have fully accepted the view that the French language has lost its competition with English for status as an international language. This perception might explain why university students who enroll in foreign language classes do so because of internal factors (personal attitudes and experiences) rather than because of external factors (social value). Another possible explanation is that most first-year students in this sample were between 18 and 19 years old and as such may not yet have developed a well-defined idea of what kind of profession they might target. This may be due in part to not yet being well aware of the supports and resources society can offer. As Beaud (2004) states, "il est très difficile lorsque l'on a dix-huit ans de savoir si l'on va aimer le droit, la sociologie ou la psychologie" (p. 18), which translates as "it is very difficult for an 18-year-old to know if he or she is going to like law, sociology, or psychology" (authors' translation).

As students progress in their second year of studies and then in their third year (license), it is anticipated that their academic maturity will develop further in at least two ways. First, one would expect that by the second or third year of university, students might begin to get a clearer sense of their own educational and professional purposes with a more grounded view of what might be available to them professionally. This study found that second- and third-year students reported more positive attitudes toward learning a foreign language compared with first-year students. Moreover, students in each year-level cohort consistently reported a moderate degree of perceived educational and career opportunities opening up as a result of foreign language study. Second, one could also hypothesize that university language classes have a significant effect on students' attitudes toward foreign language learning. Although first-year students in this study generally reported that taking classes was a fairly important part of learning a foreign language, this perceived importance was even higher among upper-year students. In other words, while taking these classes, students became more aware of the intrinsic value of the study of foreign languages such that learning a foreign language became an end in itself corresponding to a genuine interest in the specific discipline. The findings of this study clearly showed that these internal factors seemed to play a more dominant role in explaining student motivation. The perceived opportunities remained important, but they may be progressively associated with professions for which the study of foreign languages is an end rather than merely a tool; such professions could include teaching, interpreting, translating, and working abroad for the pleasure of being in an interlinguistic context or for the love of the foreign culture.

Although the findings of this study seem quite encouraging, one of the main design limitations is that this was a cross-sectional design. As such, one can only speculate as to how a particular group of first-year students might develop their beliefs and attitudes as they progress into later years. Not unlike students in many first-year programs, not all first-year students in these universities continue to the second year of their degree. Some fail and others drop out and choose another specialization or seek employment. It is possible that those who drop out were already more strongly influenced by the social value of learning a foreign language, whereas those students who progressed into the second and third year of their studies might have begun their programs with a strong personal interest. A second limitation was that some items in the survey were either too vague or did not correspond well to the response scale, which may have made it more difficult to assess students' perceptions accurately. For example, the three items representing the social value construct referred to "foreign languages" rather than any particular language. Students might have reported higher and more consistent agreement if these questions had referred to a particular and common language such as English. In contrast, other students' responses might have been based on relatively lesser-used languages (e.g., Ukrainian), perhaps leading to the view that there is little social value to learning foreign languages. Although the ratings of personal experiences were increasingly positive from first year to third year, the scale might have enabled students to respond more meaningfully if it had been based on a range of frequencies rather than levels of agreement.

The following questions need to be raised. Do students who drop out feel that the field of foreign language learning does not correspond to what they had imagined? Is the reason for dropping out due to an increasingly negative perception of the social value of learning foreign languages? Did they, for example, become increasingly persuaded that foreign language learning might not necessarily facilitate finding employment? Did they feel that the focus of the program was perhaps not congruent with how they hoped to use foreign languages in their professional and personal lives? Did they feel that the teaching strategies were not congruent with their desire to learn to communicate in the contemporary context of an increasingly globalized world? Many written comments that the students included in open-ended questions at the end of each section of the survey expressed a certain amount of disappointment due to the perceived lack of focus on communication and oral practice in their professors' teaching methods. As well, many of these written comments expressed a certain amount of dissatisfaction about the perceived lack of connection between the university's programs in foreign

NATHALIE PIQUEMAL and ROBERT RENAUD

languages and contemporary needs for increasingly internationalized relationships. In contrast, although the results of this study do suggest that students who progress into the second and third year of their studies become increasingly interested in the study of languages themselves regardless of their potential employment value, one might ask what factors contribute most toward the development of this interest. How might teachers and policymakers better address the negative perceptions of these students as well as capitalize on the positive ones?

Our findings are congruent with Rifkin's (2000) study in that they show a relationship between beliefs and attitudes about foreign language learning and level of instruction. However, whereas Rifkin's study mainly focuses on individual learning strategies and learning styles, our study also takes into account respondents' perceptions of the social value of foreign language learning. Although many of the factors used in our survey differ from those used in Rifkin's study, a common finding between these two studies is that language instruction may have a significant effect on the evolution of students' beliefs and attitudes toward foreign language learning. In contrast to Horwitz's (1988) study on the Beliefs About Language Learning Inventory (BALLI) with a group of US students from the University of Texas, our findings show that French students have a significant level of both instrumental and integrative motivation, meaning that perhaps in contrast to American students from that particular university, students in France judge that their heritage language (French for the most part) is not sufficient in the context of an increasingly globalized world that is perceived to be dominated by English as an international language. This could also explain why in our survey results, the factor *perceived opportunities* received a consistently high rating. In the current context that positions English as an international language, perceived opportunities are likely to constitute a more important factor in non-English-speakers' decision to learn foreign languages (one of which in France is generally English) than for native English-speakers. As in Gardner and Lambert's (1959) study of Canadian students, French students appear to exhibit elements of both integrative and instrumental motivations, in that perceived opportunities (PO), learning contexts (TC), and desire to identify and communicate with the new linguistic community (PA2, PA3, PE1) all received high ratings. However, our findings mainly point to an evolution between external and internal factors, with special attention to a relatively unexplored factor in foreign language research, namely, the social value of foreign language learning. More specifically, our findings suggest that the external and internal reasons for learning a foreign language become increasingly divergent as students progress from their first year of language classes into their second.

Factors that promote foreign language learning are twofold: a genuine interest in foreign languages as a field of study, and the perceived social value most probably associated with perceived opportunities. Factors that discourage foreign language learning are probably related to a decreasing perception of society's value for learning a foreign language as students progress in their studies. Faculties of foreign language studies might generate more positive attitudes in their students if they built their programs around the notion of foreign language learning as a social value important in the context of an increasingly globalized world, with both a cultural and a practical and utilitarian dimension. Given that there is an apparent evolution in students' beliefs and attitudes as they progress beyond the first year of their studies, further research should be conducted to try to tease out what exactly these perceptions are and how, qualitatively speaking, they evolve from year 1 to year 2 and year 3. It would also be interesting to compare the evolution of such beliefs and attitudes with those of students who are not involved in foreign language learning. This could help determine the degree to which these types of beliefs and attitudes exist in other disciplines.

Teachers of English as a foreign language in France need to keep in mind that their students enter their classes with both instrumental and integrative motivations. As such, the communicative aspect of foreign language learning associated with cultural learning is key in ensuring direct relevance in professional settings, as well as facilitating cross-cultural understanding and communication. How teachers can better ensure oral practice of foreign languages as well as communication in contemporary contexts needs to be explored. Teachers should invite a dialogue that helps students position themselves in the role that they might play both professionally and humanistically as the need for a lingua franca becomes increasingly paramount, and as the need to respond to linguistic and cultural diversity within and beyond our borders increases. Conversely, teachers of foreign languages in North America, and in Canada in particular, need to keep in mind the danger of succumbing to the temptations of linguistic isolationism, as well as to the imperialist tendency to impose our own linguistic model on the rest of the world. The attacks of 9/11 remind us of the myth of the developed world as a fortress, be it linguistic, economic, or political, and thus recall of the importance of learning foreign languages in attempting to develop positive and reciprocal relationships with the rest of the world.

Acknowledgments

A version of this article was presented at the 12th World Congress on Comparative Education in Havana, Cuba, October 25-29, 2004.

The authors thank the following for facilitating access to foreign language departments and classes: Université du Var à Toulon, UFR de Lettres et de Sciences Humaines, Université de Provence à Aix, Département d'Etudes du Monde Anglophone, Université de Perpignan, UFR de Lettres, Langues et Sciences Humaines, Département de LEA, Université de Perpignan, UFR de Lettres, Langues et Sciences Humaines, Département de LLCE, Université Paris-Sorbonne, Paris IV, UFR de LEA.

The authors also thank the Social Science and Humanities Research Council of Canada for funding much of the research on which this article is based.

The Authors

Nathalie Piquemal earned a doctorate in education and anthropology from the University of Alberta in 1999. She is an assistant professor in the Faculty of Education in the University of Manitoba. Her research interests include cross-cultural education, research ethics, and social contexts of foreign language learning.

Robert Renaud earned a doctorate in psychology from the University of Western Ontario in 2002. He currently teaches educational psychology, research methods, program evaluation, and advanced quantitative methods. His research interests include performance indicators, critical thinking, and quantitative methods.

References

Ashworth, M. (1985). *Beyond methodology: Second language teaching and the community.* Cambridge, UK: Cambridge University Press.

Beaud, S. (2004). Le bac est-il encore un passeport pour le futur? *La Provence.* 4 Avril.

Byrne, B.M. (2001). *Structural equation modeling with AMOS: Basic concepts, applications, and programming.* Mahwah, NJ: Erlbaum.

Calvet, L.J. (1999). *Pour une écologie des langues du monde.* Paris: Plon.

Demmert, W.G., Jr. (1993). Language, learning and national goals: A Native American view. *The issues of language and culture: Proceedings of a symposium.* Washington, CD: Center for Applied Linguistics.

Dörnyei, Z. (2003). Attitudes, orientations, and motivations in language learning: Advances in theory, research, and applications. *Language Learning, 53*(1), 3-32.

Fishbein, M., & Ajzen, I. (1975). *Belief, attitude, intention and behavior: An introduction to theory and research.* Reading, MA: Addison-Wesley.

Gardner, R.C. (1985). *Social psychology aspects of second language learning: The role of attitudes and motivation.* London: Arnold.

Gardner, R.C., & Lambert, W.E. (1959). Motivational variables in second language acquisition. *Canadian Journal of Psychology, 13*, 266-272.

Gardner, R.C., & Lambert, W.E. (1972). *Attitudes and motivations in second language learning.* Rowley, MA: Newbury House.

Graham, C.R., & Brown, C. (1996). The effects of acculturation on second language proficiency in a community with a two-way bilingual program. *Bilingual Research Journal, 20*, 235-260.

Goldin, M.G. (1987). Why Johnny can't acquire Spanish. *Hispania, 70*, 650-654.

Gumperz, J., & Hymes, D. (Eds.). (1972). *Directions in sociolinguistics.* New York: Holt, Rinehart and Winston.

Hagège, C. (1996). *Le français, histoire d'un combat.* Paris: Editions Michel Hagège.

Horwitz, E.K. (1988). The beliefs about language learning of beginning university foreign language students. *Modern Language Journal, 72*, 283-293.

Horwitz, E.K. (1991). *Language anxiety. From theory and research to classroom implications.* Englewood Cliffs, NJ: Prentice Hall.

Hu, L.-T., & Bentler, P.M. (1999). Cutoff criteria for fit indexes in covariance structure analysis: Conventional criteria versus new alternatives. *Structural Equation Modeling: A Multidisciplinary Journal, 6*, 1-55.

Hymes, D. (1972). Models of the interaction of language and social life. In J. Gumperz & D. Hymes (Eds.), *Directions in sociolinguistics.* New York: Holt, Rinehart and Winston.

Jernigan, C.G. (2001). The role of beliefs, attributions, and perceived goal attainment in students' motivation. In G. Bräuer (Ed.), *Pedagogy of language learning in higher education* (pp. 23-45). Westport, CT: Ablex.

Kamhi-Stein, L.D. (2003). Reading in two languages: How attitudes toward home language and beliefs about reading affect the behaviors of "underprepared" L2 college readers. *TESOL Quarterly, 37*, 35-71.

Kasuya, K. (2001). Discourses of linguistice dominance: A historical consideration of French language ideology. *International Review of Education, 47*, 235-251.

Kern, R.G. (1995). Students' beliefs and teachers' beliefs about language learning. *Foreign Language Annals, 28*, 71-92.

Lang, J. (2001, January 29). Minister of Education, France, Speech. (http://www/education.gouv.fr/discours/2001/dlangviv.htm.p.10). www.education.gove.fr/thema/langue/langueb2.htm)

MacIntyre, P., & Gardner, R. (1994). How does language anxiety affect second language learning? A reply to Sparks and Ganschow. *Modern Language Journal, 79*, 90-99.

Mantle-Bromley, C. (1995). Positive attitudes and realistic beliefs: Links to proficiency. *Modern Language Journal, 79*, 372-386.

Martin, I. (1990). Vocabulary acquisition in a content-based approach. *Guidelines, 12*(2), 1-11.

Masgoret, A.M., & Gardner, R.C. (2003). Attitudes, motivation, and second language learning: A meta-analysis of studies conducted by Gardner and associates. *Language Learning, 53*(1), 167-207.

Miele, P. (1982). *Suggestopedia: Easier learning the natural way*. Sandy Spring, MD: Utopia Unlimited.

Norton, B., & Toohey, K. (2001). Changing perspectives on good language learners. *TESOL Quarterly, 35*, 307-322.

Oxford, R.L. (1990). *Language learning strategies: What every teacher should know*. New York: Newbury House.

Pennycook, A. (1994). *The cultural politics of English as an international language*. London: Longman.

Rifkin, B. (2000). Revisiting beliefs about foreign language learning. *Foreign Language Annals, 33*, 394-420.

Rogoff, B. (1994). Developing understanding of the idea of communities of learners. *Mind, Culture and Activity, 1*, 209-229.

Strevens, P. (1978). The nature of language teaching. In R.C. Richards (Ed.), *Understanding second and foreign language learning: Issues and approaches* (pp. 179-203). Rowley: Newbury House.

Turner, P.R. (1974). Why Johnny doesn't want to learn a foreign language. *Modern Language Journal, 58*, 155-196.

Appendix

Complete wording of items from the questionnaire
"Social-suggestive norms in foreign language learning"

Social Value

SV1 There are government policies which encourage the French to learn foreign languages

SV2 French people believe that learning foreign languages is just a normal part of life

SV3 French people are becoming more interested in learning a foreign language

Perceived Opportunities

PO1 People who can use more than one language have more educational opportunities than those who do not

PO2 I often see job advertisements asking for people who speak more than one language

PO3 I need to learn a foreign language to get a good job

Taking Classes

TC1 For people learning a foreign language at a beginning level, foreign language classes are important

TC2 For people learning a foreign language at an intermediate level, foreign language classes are important

TC3 For people learning a foreign language at an advanced level, foreign language classes are important

Personal Attitudes

PA1 Foreign language learning is an interesting activity

PA2 It is important to learn a foreign language and culture together

PA3 I would like to learn a foreign language so that I can get to know its speakers better (BALLI)

Personal Experience

PE1 I often try to communicate with people who speak the language I am learning

PE2 I often read the newspaper in a foreign language

In the Classroom/En classe

Teachers as Learners in the ESL Classroom: It's old news, but it's news to me

Justine Light

In this article, an ESL instructor reflects on her preconceptions of power and control in the classroom. In the community-based program described, learners determined not only when and where classes would take place, but also the aims, curriculum, and content of the program. The challenges of this setting required the instructor to redefine her role in the classroom. After pursuing a more thorough review of the literterure, the author hegan to realize that she had come upon a model that is not new and is part of a well-established tradition of participatory learning.

Cet article porte sur la réflexion d'une enseignante en ALS sur ses idées précon-çues relatives au pouvoir et au contrôle dans la salle de classe. Dans le programme communautaire que l'on décrit, ce sont les apprenants qui déterminaient non seulement quand et où les cours allaient se donner, mais aussi les objectifs, le contenu et le programme d'études. Devant le défi que posait ce contexte, l'ensei-gnante a dû repenser son rôle dans la salle de classe. Après s'être penchée davantage sur la recherche portant sur ce sujet, l'auteure s'est rendu compte qu'elle était tombée sur un modèle qui n'était pas nouveau, mais qui, en fait, faisait partie de la tradition bien établie de la pédagogie active.

Introduction

In this article, I examine my journey of self-discovery through a community-based ESL program to a new understanding of power and position in the classroom. The journey began in a community-based literacy program in Edmonton. My students led me to a new place of understanding my role in the classroom and a new collaborative, negotiated model of ESL instruction. At the conclusion of the program, I turned to the literature to reflect on my experiences, which I had recorded every week in a journal format on the reverse of each lesson plan. It turns out that my discovery was old news and part of a rich tradition of collaborative community-based models.

Background to the Program

In early 2003, I began work in a program coordinated by an immigrant-serving agency in response to requests from some ethnocultural groups in the city for heritage language instruction for their children. The Edmonton Public School Board and Edmonton Catholic School District offer a number of heritage language programs including Ukrainian, German, Spanish, and Mandarin. However, for newer immigrants to Edmonton whose populations may be smaller, programs are not currently available despite strong demand. In addition, parents from these groups wished to learn more about and better understand the Canadian education system, its expectations, and communication with parents. The program, which began in early 2003, comprised a language teacher from the community who would provide heritage language instruction to school-aged children. At the same time, parents, predominantly mothers at the outset, would participate in an ESL class focused on literacy for which I was to be the instructor. The program was to take place in a community setting away from the immigrant-serving agency and was to be entirely run by the community groups who had initiated it.

"Big Ticket Items"

The class that I faced on that first Saturday in March was made up of 14 women with diverse educational and literacy backgrounds all from the Somali-Canadian community. The aims of the program had been described to me as improving communication in families and between families and their children's community. I had determined that given the unique needs expressed by the community about learning about the school system in Canada and the range of literacy levels in the group, I would take a content-based approach, focusing on as many as possible published sources that were available for parents from the school districts in the city. Beyond this decision, the program was entirely led by the students. The community group administered the program and was to determine (in consultation with the students) all aspects of the class. These included the details of a practical nature: where the classes would be held, the day and time of the classes, and how long the classes would be. However, the challenge to my own views of teaching ESL did not come from these surface details. It came from a fundamental shift that took place in this class. I would have to give up control over what Nunan (1999) refers to as the "big ticket items." By this I mean that responsibility for program aims, curriculum, and content were to be almost entirely determined by the community group.

Content and Curriculum

Each week the learners would indicate the content areas about which they were interested in learning. These included talking to your child's teacher, understanding school expectations for behavior, issues facing immigrant and ESL youth, Edmonton Public Libraries' summer reading program, understanding provincial test results, and questions you could ask at your child's school. I would then attempt to find written materials about the subject area. School boards produce a large quantity of materials that are continually updated. These materials were then in some cases abridged to enable the literacy students to access them. In other cases, as in the case of school newsletters and report cards, the original texts were maintained. The students then participated in activities familiar to many ESL teachers: reading comprehension, vocabulary development, and basic writing exercises. I drew heavily on the *Canadian Language Benchmarks for Literacy* (2000) to provide structure to the skills and to develop materials as the group worked through the content. As the group developed closer bonds, more issues were raised such as bullying, exclusions from school, and special needs classes for us to pursue. In the weeks following the initial discussion of an issue, I brought in materials related to these topics. As the group grew in confidence and determined which questions they wanted answered, the community invited outside speakers. These included principals from the Public and Catholic School Boards, an ESL consultant, and a university academic. The students were not only keen to hear what these experts had to say, but also wanted dialogue. We spent considerable time in class brainstorming questions to which the students wanted answers. Also, the group prepared a statement for each expert about what they expected from the Canadian education system.

The lack of control over the curriculum and content was a new experience for me as an ESL teacher. Previous contexts required teachers to follow a wide range of curricula focusing on various themes, settings, and functions. However, I had ultimately maintained control over the order in which things were completed, what could be comfortably omitted, and what required more time in order to avoid confusion. In this new context, I was continually challenged by the learners to satisfy their interests. I could not rely on carefully preconstructed ESL materials and textbooks and became largely responsible for creating all the materials used in class.

A further adaptation for me was that some of the ideas I proposed were rejected as uninteresting or irrelevant. One example involved looking at the publications from a school in the city that had a large Native enrollment. As an ESL expert, I found the materials highly accessible with straightforward language that avoided educational jargon. There was a firm refusal to consider the materials in the classroom as the students felt that the texts did not directly address the needs of immigrant children. They felt empowered to question the use of these materials. However, if faced with this situation again, I would argue more forcefully for their inclusion. The paradox of the learner-centered classroom was not lost on me. The curriculum should not be designed solely by me, but had to be negotiated to include the most important aspects of my personal "pedagogical agenda" (Nunan, 1999, p. 16). Auerbach (2000) noted that the teacher is at the center of every classroom and that the effort to enable more participatory learning maintains this central role for the teacher. This follow-up review of the literature continues to clarify this complex issue for me.

The Ultimate Arbiter of Meaning

My perspective on what a learner-centered methodology involved had been a rather vague understanding that learners would have some control over the classroom process. My experience of teaching ESL/EFL in the United Kingdom and Canada has been that despite my genuine efforts to establish learner-centered classrooms, I have comfortably maintained my status as what Nunan (1999) calls the "ultimate arbiter of meaning." The next professional challenge forced on me during this community-based experience was to challenge this preconceived position. Despite my academic mentors' best efforts to introduce the ideas of Willis (1996), Nunan (1999), and the vast educational literature that demands that teachers assume the role of facilitator, guide, and learner among learners, it was this literacy program that forced me to face the need for this reality.

The program had been assigned a coordinator from the community who was responsible for negotiating the demands of the students, relaying them to me, and providing feedback. It was established from the outset that the coordinator would sit in on the classes. In the early days, she helped to communicate the learners' concerns and questions and provide them with support. The conversations in class often switched to the learners' L1, a decision that reflected the learners' response to their need to discuss the real challenges faced by their children every day. Many ESL teachers can relate to the feedback I received when I asked for a summary of the highly animated conversation that had taken place: "Nothing, teacher. We fixed it." There was more to this context than the monolingual teacher in a bilingual classroom. It became apparent early that the coordinator was the person to whom the learners looked for answers to all their questions. I became acutely aware that I would be the facilitator and guide and that although I had expertise that my students expected, I would have equal partners in the classroom. The learners themselves, acutely aware of their own needs, formed a partnership first with the program coordinator, who had a linguistic and educational foot in her community and the broader Canadian experience. As the instructor with access and expertise to develop materials and activities to promote literacy, I formed the third partner.

Building a meaningful relationship with the community coordinator became a priority. This classroom partner was a rich resource who genuinely took responsibility for liaison in the class. As we worked together more closely, we grew to trust each other. She recognized that I was responding to the requests of students, and I understood that I could fulfill my role as facilitator better with her than without her.

Another surprise came toward the end of the program. During the month of Ramadan, the women in the community felt that it would be too demanding to attend school on Saturday while having to prepare the evening meal. I was then informed that this would be the opportunity for the fathers from the community to participate in the program for its remaining six weeks. This switch required a complete change of approach as the literacy needs of these learners were quite different. We had to start building trust again, although thanks to our reputation, we did not start again at zero. The atmosphere in the group was quite different, and once again I had little input into the decision that would radically change the classroom experience.

Building Trust in a New Paradigm

At this point, I realized that although the contexts of teaching ESL earlier in my life had appeared to vary greatly (different institutions, curricula, textbooks, and supervisors), it was in fact a grand illusion. In this new context, I realized that I had shifted to a new role as an ESL instructor, a role in which power was no longer the rightful prerogative of the teacher, but was shared by all participants in the experience we were creating together. The class was based in an urban area where a high density of the ethnocultural community lived, worked, and attended school. The classroom was in a community support home; we worked in the kitchen area. Many of the learners knew one another before the class began; they shared experiences, language, and religion. One of the enduring strengths of community-based endeavors is the commonality of participants and the resulting focus on the requirements of the group (Morgan, 2002). For the first time in my professional career, I was the outsider, the newcomer to the community. It was not clear what would be expected of me. I was unsure of the social rules that would silently govern the classroom interaction. I would rely on the generosity of the learners and their community leader to draw me in. The new roles would require me to become a teacher-student and my students to participate as teachers (Freire, 1973). The process of this classroom setting would be a challenge to what Freire described as the vertical pattern of classroom power. It would require all participants to teach one another.

To date I have enjoyed my career as an ESL teacher. In addition to expertise in my subject area and pedagogical approach, I have relied on rapport with my students that has blossomed into trust and mutual respect in every context in which I have worked. My experiences in the first two months of this new ESL position forced me to question and reflect on all this experience. It was difficult to develop rapport and trust. I was not the center of the classroom. I could not assume that students would look to me to interpret their questions and needs. Often it seemed as if conversations of real interest were taking place in a language in which I was unable to participate. Trust evolved differently. As mutual respect and trust among the students began to develop, and as the coordinator and I began to communicate and locate our shared interests, a rapport developed that was more substantial and entirely mutual.

Program Successes

I would be remiss to reflect on the profound effect this program had on my own understanding of being a professional ESL teacher if I did not pause to consider the successes of the program for the learners and their community. The program contributed to learners' confidence in handling the vast quantities of written materials that are presented to parents by schools. My preliminary viewing of the post-test assessments revealed an increase in understanding of educational vocabulary and the discourse of teachers and administrators. The learners had experienced the empowerment that comes with sharing their concerns, finding that others share the same concerns, and then working to find collective solutions. My experience confirmed what Auerbach (2000) noted: the strong sense of community control over *turf* and content that had emboldened the learners and enabled them to focus entirely on the issues they had collectively prioritized. Auerbach theorized that teachers and learners may have to become allied activists for change, and this happened when the program coordinator and I attended an education policy standing committee held at the legislative building in which ESL issues were discussed in an open session. In this way, the community established some useful connections to educators and has reached out into the wider community. These links will outlast the program itself and are the beginnings of a network. The success of the program can clearly be attributed to the community, and in the community there has been a flurry of activity to organize and fund other programs.

How is This Context Really Different for an ESL Teacher?

As I developed this article, I considered whether the differences that were apparent in this particular context of ESL teaching were more imagined than real. Many ESL teachers are required to negotiate their power relationships and participate in negotiated curricula. Why had this experience felt so challenging and distinctive? The differences center on how my role as an ESL professional was challenged. This program provided the ideal context for realizing the theoretical model that cast me as the guide and an equal partner in the group. Compounding this was an initial feeling that my expertise was not valued in the program. At the outset of the program, students rejected ideas that I presented and demanded texts that I felt were too challenging. This was not a positive classroom setting for me. What took place over the course of the program was negotiation. As my relationship with the program coordinator grew, I was able to show her that my experience was valuable in structuring the students' demands and maintaining their motivation and interest. I was acutely aware that these students did not want a repeat of LINC classes and that they were able to define their own goals. Nunan's (1999) caveat that learner-centered instruction "is not a matter of handing over rights and powers to learners in a unilateral way" (p. 12) became an important guidepost for me. My students were motivated and knew their objectives, but I too had an important role in guiding them to achieve these objectives.

The second major challenge to my role as an ESL professional was the seemingly unwieldy nature of managing the curriculum. The curriculum was not predetermined because of its collaborative nature; it was dynamic. The workload was intense due largely to the role of the learners in determining content and objectives. The units of study were constantly changing, and at times it felt impossible to achieve coherence. As the instructor, however, I benefited greatly from the high level of interest and motivation that the students showed for everything we covered. The unity of the group was greatly enhanced as time passed, with a continual overlap of students' interests and the curriculum.

Every challenge in this teaching context enabled me to reorient myself as an ESL professional. The challenges motivated me to try some of the theoretical constructs I had been reading about in my master's program, to manipulate them, and to appraise critically how well they functioned. This program was a perfect fit for a graduate student. I taught only two hours a week, so I had time to reflect on how theory could affect the classroom. Furthermore, I was not subjected to the pressures of a practicum with its observations and artificial classroom relationships, historically viewed as a place to compare theory and practice. Perhaps most important, I was given the opportunity to experience for a few weeks the reality of marginalization. I worked hard for acceptance by the group, and this experience will be part of who I am as an ESL teacher.

Success in this setting demands that teachers understand their role in the classroom and with the community and its leaders. Learning about the community one will be working with, their experiences, and needs, can be a valuable investment of time. Morgan (2002) provides a critical definition of the pedagogy of community-based ESL, which "implies a way of teaching in which social concerns are conceived of as equal to and somewhat prior to linguistic ones" (p. 149). His definition reveals how teachers' expertise and community needs become inextricably linked, giving value to what both parties bring to the process. ESL professionals in this setting are required to be flexible. After the initial shock to my teaching system, I came to embrace the active role my students took in their own learning. I determined that they needed decoding strategies and abridged materials, but they knew that understanding the social discourse of Canadian schools was critical to them.

It is a truly memorable moment for a teacher to facilitate learning in a context independently defined and engaged in by the learner.

In conclusion, the ESL professional in a setting such as that described here must remember to bring expertise to the process. The students in a community-based program are part of a process in which power is shared and curriculum is negotiated, but he teacher must trust his or her instincts. I experienced a fundamental shift during this program in my understanding of what being an ESL professional means. It felt as if the ground had shifted beneath me. After pursuing a more thorough review of the literature, I began to realize that I had found a model that is not new. Participatory education is a widely accepted model (Auerbach, 1996). I had discovered something through my students, and I was able to realize fully the meaning of a learner-centered classroom where learners would contribute the curriculum and language learning activities. I recognize the value of my new responsibility. A professional teacher is first and foremost a learner. It is not only new techniques and language acquisition theories to which I must remain receptive. Challenging my own assumptions about a teacher's role in the ESL classroom continues to be the greatest challenge in my professional development.

Acknowledgments

I thank Virginia Sauvé, Jaye Fredrickson, and Leila Ranta for their insightful comments on earlier versions of this article.

The Author

Justine Light has taught ESL in the UK and Canada. She is currently working as an ESL instructor at NorQuest College in Edmonton and is the President-Elect of ATESL.

References

Auerbach, E. (1996). *Adult ESL/Literacy from the community to the community: A guidebook for participatory literacy training.* Englewood Cliffs, NJ: Erlbaum.

Auerbach, E.R. (2000). Creating participatory learning communities: Paradoxes and possibilities. In J.K. Hall & W.G. Eggington (Eds.), *The sociopolitics of English language teaching* (pp. 143-164). Clevedon, UK: Multilingual Matters.

Freire, P. (1973). *Pedagogy of the oppressed.* New York: Continuum.

Johansson, L. et al. (2000). *Canadian language benchmarks 2000: ESL for literacy learners.* Ottawa: Canadian Language Benchmarks.

Morgan, B. (2002). Critical practice in community based ESL programs: A Canadian perspective. *Journal of Language, Identity and Education, 1,* 141-162.

Nunan, D. (1999). *Second language teaching and learning.* Boston, MA: Heinle & Heinle.

Willis, J. (1996). *A framework for task-based learning.* Harlow, UK. Longman.

Book Reviews / Comptes rendus

Topics in Language and Culture for Teachers
Steven Brown and Jodi Eisterhold
Ann Arbour, MI: University of Michigan Press, 2004, 211 pages
ISBN: 0-472-08916-1

Teaching in today's classroom demands teachers' attention to the unique needs of linguistically and culturally diverse learners. Some preservice and inservice teachers may feel confident and capable in facing this challenge; however, many others, particularly those experiencing diversity for the first time, may feel uncertain and unprepared as they enter this foreign landscape. Steven Brown and Jodi Eisterhold's book *Topics in Language and Culture for Teachers* explores the intersection of language and culture and offers teachers an initial passage into the world of linguistic and cultural diversity.

The authors have targeted preservice teachers as their primary audience, although *Topics in Language and Culture for Teachers* would also be a beneficial resource for inservice teachers. Both groups of teachers would be well served by the authors' vast knowledge and experience of diverse teaching and learning environments that infuses their text. My professional background in academic English language programs leads me to further recommend this book as a supplemental reading text for use in academic English language classrooms.

Brown and Eisterhold must be congratulated for producing a well-organized, and highly user-friendly book. As well as offering 11 distinct yet interconnected chapters, there are three practical, relevant appendices: (a) a listing and brief description of language families, (b) an introduction to the fundamentals of linguistics, and (c) a categorized list of journals and professional associations. The chapters in *Topics in Language and Culture for Teachers* are pedagogically sound from a reading perspective, with appropriate pre-reading and post-reading sections. The pre-reading exercises presented at the beginning of each chapter allow teachers/learners to draw on previous knowledge and to reflect on their existing beliefs about the concepts that are addressed in that chapter. The chapter readings are clearly written, supported by pertinent research without delving too deeply, and they provide an invaluable introduction to, and overview of, the significant concepts, topics, and issues surrounding language and culture including the nature of language and culture, language and interaction, first-language acquisition, second-language learning, varieties of language, nonverbal communication, sign languages, and literacy. Each chapter ends with a variety of post-read-

JOAN BIRRELL-BERTRAND and ELLEN PILON

ing activities and a short list of suggested readings that give course instructors or independent learners choices for follow-up to the information addressed in the chapter.

Although all the chapter activities have practical value, I was particularly impressed with the "Teaching Scenario" and the "Reflect" elements of each chapter. The "Teaching Scenarios" contextualize the specific focus of the chapter in a classroom scenario through which the teachers/learners can consider and discuss possible approaches to the situation. For example, in Chapter Seven "Language Contact between Individuals and Cultures," one scenario invites teachers/learners to consider English-only speaking policies in a classroom with many immigrant students. The authors present such questions as "What are the possible group (not individual) consequences of this policy? Is the policy a good one? Does the language(s) the immigrants speak factor into your answer?" (p. 114) as a guide to discussing this common scenario. Similarly, the "Reflect" component of each chapter provides teachers/learners with an opportunity to consider their personal professional practice and how this might be influenced by their increasing awareness of language and culture issues. Brown and Eisterhold's inclusion of these sections firmly grounds the theoretical content in the realm of classroom practice.

Another real strength of *Topics in Language and Culture for Teachers* is the authors' recognition of the significance and place of technology in education. To this end, some of the chapter exercises and activities incorporate the use of films or film clips and the Internet. Although the films or film clips would probably be incorporated into class time, the use of the Internet offers learners the opportunity to enhance and extend their knowledge through further study outside class time.

Finally, I commend Brown and Eisterhold for wisely and gently introducing and discussing the topics of generalization and stereotypes in Chapter One. Considering that their book is specifically designed for teachers with no background knowledge in linguistics, anthropology, or cultural studies, it is sensible to explore such critical issues as ethnocentrism and deficit models immediately and directly. The authors embrace the belief that diversity should be seen as a positive, a message that is reinforced throughout the text and one that may resonate with teachers as they weave together their newly acquired background knowledge with their classroom experiences.

Clearly there is much to celebrate in the arrival of *Topics in Language and Culture for Teachers,* for it is an excellent starting place to address the diversity present in classrooms today. Whether as a course textbook for preservice teachers, as a professional resource tool for inservice teachers, or as a reading text in academic English language contexts, this book offers a way of increasing awareness of, gaining insight into, and preparing for linguistic and cultural diversity within classroom environments.

Joan Birrell-Bertrand

The Reviewer
Joan Birrell-Bertrand has been involved with ESL/EFL for children, youth, and adults in Canada and overseas for the past 14 years. Her various teaching roles include English for academic purposes, content-based English language instruction, and teacher training in the CTESL program at the University of Manitoba. Currently Joan is the editorial assistant for the *TESL Canada Journal.*

Sociolinguistic Variation and Change
Peter Trudgill
Washington, DC: Georgetown University Press, 2002, 197 pages

Peter Trudgill is a name any researcher in sociolinguistics, linguistics, or dialects will encounter. In the book's references he is listed 28 times as either sole author or co-author of publications. For more than 30 years, he has studied sociolinguistics and is knowledgeable about dialects all over the world, including one just outside Lunenburg, Nova Scotia. The book jacket tells us that he "is currently working on the British Isles dialect origins of New Zealand English, and on the lesser-known native-speaker varieties of English around the world."

This book is a selection of Trudgill's work published elsewhere between 1988 and 2000, mostly in journals, and revised for this publication. Therefore, although it repeats some of the ideas in his other books, it is not a reprint of chapters from them. Rather it is an encapsulation divided into five sections: Sociohistorical linguistics, Dialect change, Language contact, Language creation and language death, and Englishes. Each chapter of each section builds on his prior studies, but raises interesting questions that could yet be researched. Graduate students in sociolinguistics could find interesting dissertation ideas in these chapters. Prior knowledge of sociolinguistics or at the very least its terminology, would assist the reader in understanding the content, especially of the first half of the book.

Each chapter is filled with a wealth of fascinating detail and ideas that stimulate the reader. For example, in chapter 5, Trudgill gives a characteristic of modern NZ English, the "disyallabic pronunciation of past participles such as sown, grown, known so that they rhyme with Owen" (p. 41). The section Language Contact delves into pidgins and creoles: how they evolve and how they develop. We learn that "whenever adults and post-adolescents learn a new language, pidginisation takes place" (p. 68). Pidginization has three processes: reduction, admixture and simplification. In chapter 8 we learn about linguistic gender: why it occurs and why it is omitted in pidgins. We learn that there is no morphology in pidgin.

JOAN BIRRELL-BERTRAND and ELLEN PILON

Trudgill touches on historical and sociolinguistic connections between some different varieties of English, such as "do" in East Anglian dialect and in African American Vernacular English, and short "o" in East Anglia and New England. He covers dedialectalization and dialect death. Dialects are important, he says, because they reinforce local cultures and local identities, and they counter nationalism. Dialect loss is partly attributable to attitudes and bias where nonstandard language is considered inferior. In chapter 10 we review dialects where third person "s" is omitted.

The final sections are perhaps most interesting in the light of current research into world English. Trudgill identifies Abstand and Ausbau languages. Abstand is a linguistic variety that is a language in its own right because it is at a linguistic distance; an example is Basque. An Asbau language, on the other hand, is a linguistic variety considered a language in its own right because of cultural or political reasons. For example, Ukrainian and Belorussion are languages, although the two countries have had difficulties in maintaining that their languages are distinct from Russian. In the chapters on language death, Trudgill voices strong opinions. "Any language, however, has the capacity to be a killer language" (p. 140). English is a killer language, but so is Spanish, which is a threat to hundreds of languages in Central and South America. Trudgill is clearly in favor of language diversity and against linguistic and cultural homogenization. "Barriers to communication are a Good Thing" (p. 143), he asserts. He points out that if everyone in the world spoke the same language, it would be a very boring and uniform place.

The last section, Englishes, touches on an aspect of interest to all English-language teachers: standard English. Trudgill identifies two linguistic catastrophes that might befall the English language. One is the Americanization catastrophe, which is attributable to the widespread influence of the US electronic media. The other is the disintegration catastrophe: English is spoken so widely worldwide that it might break into "mutually unintelligible dialects" (p. 148). He suggests that changes in English are largely lexical; grammatical change is much slower. Finally, he asserts that standard English is only one variety of English among many, but that it remains the most important because it is used by most educated people. Standard English is not a language, an accent, a style, or a register; it is a social dialect and the one that we teach. In his final chapter, he argues that Received Pronunciation (RP) is the preferred accent for English instruction.

Sociolinguistic Variation and Change will appeal to any academic reader interested in how English has grown and changed worldwide. It is a taste of sociolinguistics and dialect studies sure to prod the reader into reading more books by Peter Trudgill.

Ellen Pilon

The Reviewer
Ellen Pilon is a senior ESL teacher at the International Language Institute in Halifax, NS. She has an MA (English), an MLS, and an MEd TESL and delights in reading new books.

Master's Program in TESL

Mount Saint Vincent University, in co-operation with Saint Mary's University, offers the **Master of Education in Curriculum Studies: TESL** program. Students can complete the full-time degree in eight months, or on a part-time basis.

Program information and admission requirements are available online at **www.msvu.ca/education** under **Curriculum Studies**.

Applications are available online at **www.msvu.ca/apply_online**.

For more information, please contact Jocelyne Lavoie at jocelyne.lavoie@msvu.ca or toll-free at 1-877-433-2889.

www.msvu.ca
Discover the difference.

MOUNT SAINT VINCENT UNIVERSITY
Excellence · Innovation · Discovery

Call for Papers

The ® Clearinghouse on Languages and Linguistics invites you to submit papers, reports, curricula or other materials for inclusion in the ERIC® database.

Submissions should be sent to:
Acquisitions Coordinator ERIC/CLL
4646 40th Street NW
Washington DC 20016-1859

TEL 202-362-0700 • FAX 202-362-3740
E-MAIL eric@cal.org
Read more about including your work in ERIC at
www.cal.org/ericcll/Submitting.html

 **INTERNATIONAL ASSOCIATION OF TEACHERS OF ENGLISH AS A FOREIGN LANGUAGE**

Linking, developing and supporting English language teaching professionals worldwide

The broad aims of IATEFL are:

- To benefit English language teachers all over the world and provide teachers with opportunities for personal development
- To enable the international network of ELT professionals to grow, for example, by encouraging and fostering the regional and local groupings, so that members can learn from each other
- To encourage grassroots professionalism where all categories of members at whatever stage of their career can make significant contributions and continue to learn.

For more details, including membership application form, visit our website www.iatefl.org or contact the office on generalenquiries@iatefl.org

Darwin College
University of Kent
Canterbury
Kent
CT2 7NY
UK
00 44 (0)1227 824430

When talk is a science...

Linguistics & Language Behavior Abstracts

Comprehensive, cost-effective, timely coverage of current ideas in linguistics and language research

Abstracts of articles, books, and conference papers from more than 1,100 journals plus citations or relevant dissertations as well as books and other media.

Available in print or electronically through USA Illumina *(www.csa.com).*

Contact sales@csa.com for trial Internet access or a sample issue.

www.csa.com

TESL Canada Journal

TESL Canada Journal, established in 1984, issued twice yearly, publishes articles dealing with diverse aspects of teaching and learning of ESL/EFL, including; · syllabus design · psycholinguistics · teacher training · computer assisted learning · methodology · testing and evaluation · applied linguistics · curriculum design

Subscriptions are sold by volume only. No. 1 of each volume is mailed to you in the Fall; No. 2 is mailed in the Spring. Please do not request calendar year or split-volume subscriptions. Individual subscriptions cannot be sent to institutional addresses. Proof of student status must accompany student orders. Payment can be made by cheque, money order, VISA, Mastercard or Purchase Order payable to TESL Canada Journal.

Send to TESL Canada Journal, #408 – 4370 Dominion Street, Burnaby, B.C. V5G 4L7 Canada.
Phone 604.298.0312. Fax 604.298.0372. Email: admin@tesl.ca

TESL Canada Journal Order Form

☐ **$40** Individuals   ☐ **$60** Non-Profit Institutions   ☐ **$20** Students

Name: _____

Organization: _____

Tel.: _____ Email: _____

Address: _____

City _____ Country _____ Postal Code _____

Please add $6.00 to all Canadian, $8.00 to all U.S. and $12.00 to all overseas orders for postage. All Canadian orders must add 6% GST. All orders from outside Canada please pay in U.S. funds.

$_____ (subscription) + $_____ (GST) + $_____ (postage) = $_____

If paying by VISA or Mastercard:

Name on Card: _____ Exp. Date _____

Card # _____

For further information, please contact:
TESL Canada,
#408 – 4370 Dominion Street,
Burnaby, B.C. V5G 4L7 Canada

Telephone 604.298.0312. Fax 604.298.0372. Email admin@tesl.ca

Visit our website at www.tesl.ca for information on purchasing individual articles from the TESL Canada Journals.

TESL Canada 2008 Conference

May 29 – May 31   2008 Delta Beausejour   Moncton, NB

Uncovering Discourse

Keynote Addresses: Scott Thornbury / Jeremy Harmer

More Information: www.teslns.ca

Co-hosted by:

TESL NB — Teachers of English as a Second Language of New Brunswick

TESL ⚓ NS

TESL CANADA JOURNAL/BULLETIN

ADVERTISING RESERVATION FORM

Please reserve the following advertising space in the 2007 **SPRING ISSUE** of the TESL Canada Journal/Bulletin:

☐	**Journal**, Full Page	$300.00
☐	**Journal**, ½ Page	$200.00
☐	**Journal**, Inside Front Cover	$400.00
☐	**Journal**, Inside Back Cover	$350.00
☐	**Journal**, Outside Back Cover	$450.00
☐	**Bulletin**, Full Page	$250.00
☐	**Bulletin**, ½ Page	$150.00
☐	**Bulletin**, ¼ Page	$100.00
☐	**Bulletin**, Business Card size	$ 50.00

☐   **Insert**, Single Sheet $1000.00
     5,500 copies will be provided to the mailing house by October 1, 2006
☐   **Insert**, Catalogue   Price to be determined
     5.500 copies will be provided to the mailing house by October 1, 2006

☐   Camera ready copy is enclosed.
☐   Camera ready/electronic copy will be sent by (specify date):
_____

☐   Repeat advertisement currently on file.

My placement preference is (specific location) _____

Special instructions: _____

_____

Name of Contact: _____

Tel. No. _____   Email address: _____

Company: _____

Address: _____

Date: _____   Signature: _____

Fax to 604-298-0372 or mail to TESL Canada Advertising, 408 – 4370 Dominion Street, Burnaby, B.C. V5G 4L7 or email to admin@tesl.ca.